Resident Dormitus

Resident Dormitus

Vikas Rathi

Rupa & Co

Copyright © Vikas Rathi 2011

Published 2011 by
Rupa Publications India Pvt. Ltd.
7/16, Ansari Road, Daryaganj,
New Delhi 110 002

Sales Centres:

Allahabad Bengaluru Chennai
Hyderabad Jaipur Kathmandu
Kolkata Mumbai

All rights reserved.
No part of this publication may be reproduced, stored in a
retrieval system, or transmitted, in any form or by any means,
electronic, mechanical, photocopying, recording or otherwise,
without the prior permission of the publishers.

The author asserts the moral right to be identified
as the author of this work.

This is a work of fiction. Any resemblance to people,
places or events is purely coincidental.

Printed in India by
Rekha Printers Pvt Ltd.
A-102/1, Okhla Industrial Area, Phase-II,
New Delhi-110 020

Printed at Repro Knowledgecast Limited, Thane

Dedicated to my parents and Soumil....

... With thanks to Patricia Mathias, Sharad J. Lal, Eshan Ponnadurai, Rafael Scislowski, Karan Bajaj, V.S. Aravind, Rakhi Pandey, Hiren Gajria, Albinus Saw, Deborah Raymond, Darul Kisai, Dudette and Debika Roy Marwah.

Contents

Prologue ix

1. Resident Dormitus — 1
2. Cool and Addictive — 8
3. Welcome to the Jungle — 23
4. Living on the Edge — 37
5. Alice in Wonderland — 52
6. The Terrorist — 66
7. Lust in Work — 76
8. Self-destruction — 88
9. Mediocre but Aware — 108
10. Transmogrification — 117
11. The Grind — 124
12. The Honeymoon is Over — 133
13. Stranger at Home — 144
14. Abstinence — 153
15. To Each His Own — 160
16. Mind is Restless — 170
17. Game Over — 182

Epilogue 194

Today, a young man on acid realised that all matter is merely energy condensed to a slow vibration ... that we are all one consciousness experiencing itself subjectively. There's no such thing as death, life is only a dream, and we are the imagination of ourselves. Here's Tom with the weather.

– BILL HICKS

Prologue

'When exactly do you think we lost him?'

'At hello?' I ventured.

'Come on. For once, be serious.' Arjuna merely articulated what Alex was thinking. It had come down to that. Over the course of the longest four months of my life, we could read each other's minds without effort. The way we knew every little move the other would make, their eating habits, sleeping postures, what the raised eyebrow meant, how one's gastro-intestinal tract would behave, say, after a cappuccino, it would have put long-term couples to shame. The only competition to this sort of thing, I imagined, would be convicts sharing a prison cell and well, I wouldn't really want to go there.

When I didn't say anything, Alex put forth his own theory. 'The job must have been his undoing. A complete mismatch between his ambitions and his talent.' He leaned back and drank some beer, knowing fully well that this would ignite a debate.

'I don't know, mate. He was definitely far more talented than I am. Maybe he was just unlucky.' Arjuna registered his disagreement and looked out into the void. I had noticed the void, too; this void had come to replace what would have been filled by Dev. A year had passed since the night I last saw Dev. It had also been one year since I had met this lot. Just like our previous rendezvous, this one, too, was facilitated by an elaborate training programme which had brought us back to Singapore. This time though, it was just a week-long session and we were already through most of the week. I wondered how much these two knew of what had really transpired and I found myself fighting, for the thousandth time, the urge to confess. I emerged victorious. For the time being.

Arjuna continued, more because he was uncomfortable with long silences than anything else, 'If only you had reached on time, things could have been different.'

Arjuna's tone was clearly accusing. I gave myself a few moments to consider whether to come up with a retort, using the time to gaze over at the skyline as glimpsed from the rooftop bar. How many bars and clubs had I crawled into, those past four months and yet felt so completely out of place? Like I felt so out of place here. 'I don't think so,' I found myself saying. 'Actually, I think I was four months too early.'

'What do you mean?'

'We did really lose him at 'hello'. He was doomed the moment we entered his life.'

'At the risk of repeating myself, what do you mean?' Arjuna sounded as puzzled as he looked.

'I know what he means.' Alex was looking at me curiously. 'He means that Dev was a perfectly normal character with quirks and insecurities which he had learned to live with, by and large. Then he met us and we reminded him of what he could have been. In fact, he thought that he was already one of us, except that he couldn't make it. That did him in.'

I elaborated. 'Remember what Bala said at one of those coffee sessions – you have to be a real loser not to be able to make it. Every Tom, Dick and Harry has made it. But not Dev. You knew him. How would he have taken that kind of a rejection?'

'You may be right. One still wonders, though…if only you were there on time.' Arjuna continued on his track of wishful thinking, 'What took you so long, Achet? You said you got there only by 3 a.m.?'

'My flight got delayed,' I lied, and before I could check myself, added, 'Besides, I don't think my being there would have changed anything. He looked set to go.'

Two pairs of eyes turned to stare at me, one of them clearly more hostile than the other. The hostile pair, of course, belonged to Arjuna. 'I knew it. I just knew it, all along. I really knew I could never trust you again after that night at KL but somehow, I convinced myself you were intrinsically okay. I was wrong. You are a psychopathic murderer.' He literally spat out the last two words.

'What night at KL?' Alex asked but I cut him short. 'I am not a bloody murderer. I did what I thought was right. Or more correctly, I didn't do what I thought wasn't right.' I paused and decided to chuck some mud back at Arjuna. 'At least I didn't order somebody else to do my dirty work for me.'

Arjuna reached across and hit me, hard. For a moment or two, I couldn't feel my lower lip and then realised that it was smooshed right into my teeth. I used my tongue to disentangle the two and tasted blood.

Alex got up to restrain Arjuna and said, 'You guys are not going to fight till you bring me up to speed. There is an awful lot that I don't seem to know. After I hear all and if it is worthwhile, I promise you I will join you guys in beating each other to pulp. But not before that.' Arjuna nodded but continued to stare at me. Alex turned to me. 'Yes, Achet?'

That was when I told them the whole truth. I told them that I wasn't sorry for what I did or didn't do. I told them that it was the only way things could have gone. In fact, there was no other better way for any of us, and that included Dev. I said it all in a remorseless tone but who was I really kidding?

The point is, Dev's story could very well have been my story. In fact, there is no way I can possibly tell this tale without telling my story. Besides, I wouldn't be able to do justice to either the story or the characters for I can't possibly claim to understand what he went through. We were like the anti-particles, the positron and the electron, both of which could have happily gone on to live in their own particular universe if not brought together by chance. And, brought together, annihilation was inevitable. If I were to plot our lives on the space-time continuum, our worms came together in those four months, at the end of which one ceased to exist. To tell you the tale, I will have to go back to the day when we met.

1

Resident Dormitus

I FLEW INTO Mumbai to take up my job. I did not feel any excitement or anxiety as my internship in this company a year ago had revealed the job to be a routine one and the pay to be mediocre. I did, however, feel a sense of emptiness, because my life, as yet free and untrammelled, devoted to the solitary aim of whiling away time, seemed to be over or at least, limited now to only twelve hours a day, two-thirds of which I would spend sleeping. I had always chosen the path of least resistance, to somehow fit into the system while simultaneously ensuring the pursuit of idleness. Unfortunately, the cumulative effect of such choices was only now becoming clear to me. Like the chess player who could not think more than five moves ahead, I was now irretrievably forced along the beaten track and I could sense a premature middle age beckoning me. As I stood in line for an autorickshaw, the rainfall was not as heavy as it was back in Jaipur. In fact, it was only a slight drizzle, enough to make you uncomfortable but not nearly enough to keep you indoors. I inhaled the wet and busy smell of the city, far removed from the sleepy and laid-back air of my hometown Jaipur, tried to mesh these together to gain some illuminating insights, but in the end dismissed the thought as a philosophical luxury I could not afford.

'*Oye, chalna hai?*' inquired the stupid driver. Perhaps he thought I habitually stood in autorickshaw queues at the Mumbai airport during rainy weather without an umbrella. I was about to say this aloud but somehow felt this brand of wit might fall flat with him. Besides, I did not fancy waiting for another ride. So, I got into the rickshaw and told the man to take me to West Andheri.

'New here, sahib?' he checked.

'No, twenty-three years too old,' I said. As the driver chuckled, I quickly upgraded my earlier evaluation of his sense of humour.

We zigzagged our way through the Western Express Highway, always and forever under construction, surprisingly passed Juhu *galli* in a jiffy and reached the apartment in thirteen minutes. I had stayed here during my internship and had now been allotted a different unit in the same complex. It was quite a swanky place that consisted of three blocks of seven storeys each, massive apartments by Mumbai standards. The partly-clean, partly-soiled lift took me to the right floor and I walked into a flat containing four living humans; the fifth one seemed either dead or hibernating.

'Hi, how are you?'

'Are you also an intern?'

'Which campus are you from?'

Overwhelmed with the difficult choice of which question to answer first, I cannily added my own question to the repertoire, 'What are you guys doing here?'

After a brief commotion and the customary formalities of making more acquaintances, it turned out that these guys were all interns this year and I was to share a room with the dead guy. I was actually hoping for a room of my own after all these years. On the bright side, my roommate probably would not have much to say. I should have known better.

The apartment had a huge common area from which three doors led to three different rooms, as if somebody had purposely designed the place for both the solitary and the sociable. The spaciousness of the common area was further accentuated by two wall-sized sliding windows on either side, which in their present open state, had transformed the place into a tunnel that afforded easy passage to the ocean winds. Almost as a special effect, the curtains moved as if they had an exciting but directionless life of their own. The sparse and utterly tasteless furniture consisted of an old varnished dining table covered with a green table-cloth at one end and a wooden sofa with a coffee table at the other. The amalgamated sounds of the distant ocean, the unavoidable road traffic, children playing somewhere down below and the inevitable television white noise filled the place.

It was 7 o'clock in the evening and from the looks of it, the boys had already embarked upon the Old Monk ritual that had stood the test of time. Simply stated, it was a celebration of what was more a lucky accident than achievement of being amongst the chosen few to have arrived at the bottom rung of the mightiest corporate ladder around. Little did they realise that by the end of their internships, just about a third of them would make it; those who did not would feel denied and those who did, would feel compromised, thus spreading equal misery all around. I had been there, in just that place, exactly one year earlier, animatedly excited, the exuberance fuelled by the collected hopes of a great future mixed in with juvenile recklessness. Time, indeed, is the fourth and the most important dimension that passes at unpredictable varying speed, diagnosable only in hindsight; sometimes, one is stuck in a moment for eternity, at other times, just a seemingly trifling moment is enough for one to be irrevocably fated. In my case, one year marked the translucent one-way mirror separating myself from the interns on the other side. Though I could look back at the boys, they could not see me. It gave me an evil pleasure that I was privy to a point of view accessible only to me.

I poured a large quantity of Old Monk into a stained glass and settled down for what would inevitably be a surreal conversation.

'So you were an intern here last year. That's good. Maybe you can tell us how to convert,' said a lanky fellow whose sprawled sitting posture hid his height.

'Last year, they were recruiting just about anybody who was born in the month of April in the year 1979. I am not sure what the lucky date this time is. I hear it is highly classified,' I said in an effort to infuse the answer with humour and thereby avoid having to appear knowledgeable.

'You were born in April 1979?' asked the dead fellow as the others smiled.

'Unless they made a mistake. I thought you were dead. I am sorry to have brought you back.'

'You mean you would rather have me dead?'

'I have not made up my mind on that, as yet. I am just sorry to have brought you back from your trip.'

'It was indeed quite a trip. I need refuelling, though. I hate being alone on such trips. You look like the type. Fancy some ganja?'

'Sure,' I replied.

'Great, so I have my own resident smoking partner now. This is auspicious. I have a good feeling about the next few months. Let's roll some now.'

There were scornful glances thrown our way from the others and so we retired to a corner by the window to allow them to stay on their high horses. The not-dead guy was an expert. He had brought his own supplies of cigarette paper and weed all the way from Delhi. He unrolled the gist of his life while rolling the joint. It turned out that he, Dev Das, was twenty-eight and was doing a masters in a rare discipline with no apparent practical use, in the only university that had granted him admission. His mother was extremely disappointed in him especially, since all his peers, friends and relatives were 'well set', as the term went, in their respective careers and lives. He was extremely happy now that some company had identified his genius and apparently, he now also realised that all his life he had been inadvertently preparing for a career in management, as destiny had it. I resisted the urge to puke.

'So why did you start smoking up?' he asked.

'This is the first time I will be smoking up. How about you?'

'I do it coz of the dichotomy it offers. It's cool because it is not addictive but it is addictive because it's cool. Does that make any sense to you?' He applied spit on the cigarette paper so the joint would hold up.

'Not really,' I said. I noticed how his long hair flew about recklessly in the wind. It looked quite cool on his conventionally good-looking face. I made a mental note to grow my hair.

He lit the joint and took a drag before passing it on to me, advising me to keep it vertical lest the weed should fall out.

'You need to smoke up a bit more to be able to understand that. At least you are honest. Most folks feign complete understanding of that statement. Anyway, that is not the reason why I smoke up, though it is a good enough reason. I smoke up because it allows the dormant thoughts residing within me to resurface, thoughts that, otherwise, would have gone unheard. Is all this still nonsensical to you?'

I was having difficulty in managing the complicated task of smoking, keeping the weed within and not letting the joint extinguish itself, all at the same time. 'Multitasking is definitely not my forte,' I said, adding, 'The smell is terrible. How long does it take to hit?'

'It depends upon your receptivity. Sometimes, I need to smoke half-a-dozen. At other times, I start feeling good from the first drag itself,' he said, visibly disappointed at his audience's lack of interest in his philosophical theories.

'Well, I will get there. Back to the topic at hand. You were saying?'

'Let me give you an example. At home, my room is upstairs, slightly secluded with a window that opens out to the street in front. It provides me the privacy I need while at the same time, if I feel lonely, all I need to do is to open the window and let the street come in. Of late, I have taken to smoking pot in my room because I don't like smoking like a thief in a deserted alley at odd hours of the night. I would rather smoke at home. However, it does have its dangers, namely, getting caught. Sometimes, my mother calls me to help her with some domestic chore when I am stoned. What do I do? I push the thought of being stoned back down to the deep fathoms of my brain, come down, help her out and then go back up. And then, I retrieve that numbness again as if it was lying there in a state of cryogenic preservation. That, my friend, is what I call Resident Dormitus. Extending the analogy a bit further, during a typical numbness tour, the societal cyclical chains of happiness and angst become loose, you are able to look within and salvage the true thoughts that define you.' He took a couple of quick drags and continued, 'Have you heard of the experiment conducted by Berkeley? He summons a slave boy and merely by questioning him, makes the boy see the solution of a geometrical problem which he hadn't even known existed, thereby proving that the knowledge is resident in all human beings, yet only a few are able to realise it. Here I add my two cents: marijuana smoothens the retrieval of that knowledge.'

'It was Socrates as envisioned by Plato,' I could not help correcting him.

'And you must be the one who always looks for the credits section when reading a masterpiece. Do you want a cigarette?'

'Sure.'

In hindsight, I should have been less cynical and should have listened, really listened. The curious attribute of a revelation is that it can't be forced and often occurs post facto. It is like you will never realise that you had been warned beforehand in your horoscope till that very event which was forewarned happens. But that epiphany was still a long way off for me. There was the slippery slope to climb first.

2

Cool and Addictive

I WOKE UP with a dry mouth and realised I was running late. When one is running low on time, one usually ends up sacrificing the discretionary but important things; in my case, I had to forego breakfast, as would be the case with so many future breakfasts, too. When I left, Dev was just stirring to life in an overly-long process. On the street, I bought a cigarette from the *paan-beedi* shop, hailed an autorickshaw and sat back, smoking in a smug manner.

Outside, the cruel traffic was intruding upon the perceptibly contented sleep of the homeless who were spread out in formations similar to that of tiny ant colonies, on the roadside footpath and the road divider and wherever else they could find sufficient space in which to coil up. Some of them seemed to have been the residents of the same stretch of footpath for quite a while now, as was evident from their minor fixtures such as torn bedding. As we waited for the traffic light to turn green, I could see them performing the different phases of their morning rituals; some were brushing their teeth with their fingers, while others were on their way with overused yellowed bottles of water to what could only be the communal toilet beyond the line of sight. A cow had somehow manoeuvred its way to the road divider amidst the packed traffic and was mooing loudly, either because she was pleasantly surprised by her accomplishment and wanted the world to know about it or because she was overwhelmed by the impossibility of her situation, like the amateur mountain-climber glancing down from the peak for the first time. I observed all of it without really comprehending it, much the same way as you let cable TV wash over you in the evening, moving from one channel to another because not a single channel has the power to arrest your attention more than a few minutes at the most. I was, somehow, part of it all and yet was separated physically by the privilege of being mobile in the autorickshaw and also because I was caught up in my thoughts. It seemed to me that the sum of all probabilities somehow had zeroed upon this particular universe out of a multitude and here I was, inescapably unsure of my grounding.

My thoughts travelled back to the time when it all started. I recalled the day I was admitted into a prestigious business school in Bangalore. 'Prestigious' was the word I had used to describe my school to my friends in Jaipur and was immediately greeted with stomach-splitting laughter from them. 'So you are going to study at a prestigious business school! Which school is that? Never heard of it,' Siddhartha, who was later to become a journalist, had said. 'Can I apply to your school? Will you put in a word for me with the Dean?' To them, the world began and ended at the outskirts of Jaipur; a parochial view, it seemed to me at that time. My mother was confused about her feelings on the issue.

She was proud of my accomplishment but was unsure of what such an unexpected development meant for me. Quite possibly, she was afraid that I was going overboard in my pursuit to be considered superior to my peers and that I would be overwhelmed by all the new experiences to which I would be exposed; this perception was largely based on my emaciated physical appearance. She told me, with a rather forlorn detachment, to be true to what I really wanted and be at peace with myself. I didn't know it then and I still didn't know it yet as to what it was that I really wanted. Well, to be fair, I thought I wanted a lot of money and recognition back then but I wasn't sure of that anymore. Two years later, the story had taken a different turn. The more I tried to think about what had really changed, the more complicated it became till I started to feel dizzy. For a moment, I wondered if I was going insane but then realised it was because of the crazy way the autorickshaw was moving. It moved more sideways than forward, if that were possible, and in the process was collecting a lot of profanity reward points, bestowed upon by other fellow commuters on the road. I wondered if these rickshaw drivers compared their profanity counts at the end of the day, which would somehow determine the strength of one's manhood and consequently influence who gets to sleep with whose wife. Perhaps they even held an annual awards ceremony in which the person with the most profanities collected would be given a licence to kill on the road. I marvelled at the passion evident in the way my autorickshaw driver was driving, and speculated that I would be lucky if I could duplicate even half of it; and mine was a job that relatively paid much more handsomely, afforded interactions with like-minded smart people and had the potential to keep me intellectually curious. Then again, I mused, a licence to kill would go a long way in keeping me motivated.

It took me thirty-seven minutes to get to office. I vowed to beat the traffic in future by getting up early, a vow that I knew even at the time, I would break a thousand times. I paid for the ride and got off. It wasn't the same office where I had done my internship; it was a newly-built office in the middle of a congested and narrow one-way road, in a neighbourhood that hinted at the lower socio-economic class, clearly below the poverty line. It reeked of obscenity in much the same way that the Taj Mahal does, in that the people who built it were killed by the emperor after building it. I would later get to know that a sum of $35 million (they liked to refer to everything in dollar terms, it somehow added glamour to the work) was poured into this building and it did show. It seemed to be made of only glass and housed seven floors; all haphazardly assembled one on top of another, in a shape resembling a mushroom. Only four floors were occupied while the rest were kept ready in anticipation of hysterical growth in the future, a growth which was unlikely to happen if the past was anything to go by. There was a huge open area in front which reluctantly hosted a variety of planters, big and small, containing a maddening variety of plants and stunted trees; this was much the same manner in which the company hosted the executives upstairs. They probably didn't pay the gardener/designer person too well, a plausible result of irrational budget cuts that invariably tend to happen closer to the completion of a project. They would not bat an eyelid before investing in five-thousand-dollar office chairs but would fret about smaller things; all this eventually made the building look like a badly shaved skin-head.

I filled up the particulars in the Visitors' Book and was given a temporary visitor card. During that time, I had to bear the brunt of the security guard's questioning looks. And I didn't blame him. There were probably two types of people who came to this office: the ones who carried authority and the ones who served the authorities. I didn't look or behave like either. With an average height and with a weight that encouraged rumours about a possible escape from a Somalian refugee camp, I didn't fit into the first category; however, I also didn't look the type to submit to servitude. I had lived and mastered this dualism throughout my life simply because I didn't really have any alternative. I was born grossly underweight. The doctor said that it was because I was a premature baby though I could not understand why my mother, who was otherwise quite patient, could not wait for the right time. My parents told me that my first three years of life were characterised by a troubled medical history, wherein the number of injections I took far exceeded the bowls of milk I drank. I had always been physically weak and every sneeze of mine was regarded as a bout of something sinister. I was too afraid to take part in any sports activity and contended myself with drawing pictures, instead. Always conscious of being small, I had managed to keep a low profile, drawing as little attention to myself as possible. This included, among other things, doing my homework properly, staying in my classroom during the recess, episodes of fainting under the sun during morning assembly when my speech was due, and secretly pouring my milk down the drain when I didn't feel like drinking it.

However, all that gradually changed once the element of competition among peers was added in the act of growing up.

I realised that I had deep reserves to tap into during the times when I needed it most. I never did become the unquestionable leader at any stage or in any setting but I did manage to earn peer respect, so vital to my self-confidence. I was the only one who had managed to throw a few punches in the rare growing-up fight with another group of boys that my friends got entangled into; I paid handsomely with a swollen upper lip and a rib cage turned inside out owing to a dozen or so kicks and was also grounded for a week thereafter. But it was worth it.

In any case, I didn't really mind the security guard's scrutiny because I was used to it. In fact, I would be surprised whenever somebody considered me worthy of something at first glance, like respect at first sight. Sometimes, only sometimes, I would try my best not to prove them wrong.

I entered the building and was pleasantly greeted by the air-conditioned temperature. I was late by about nineteen minutes for the new employee welcome programme, not a bad way to start one's first day in office. I got into the lift and pressed the button for the third floor, all the while thinking of some plausible excuse to explain the delay. The receptionist showed me the way to the training room and advised me to enter from the other side, so as not to disturb whichever session was in progress. I tried to figure out the 'other side' but had to give up and enter from the only side that I could find. I opened the door, peered inside and realised that I, somehow, appeared right behind a huge burly fellow whose pants hugged his massive globular cheeks in a comical fashion; he was also conducting that particular session. I mumbled an apology, the kind of apology that is physically impossible to be heard by anyone else and which is supposed to convey the fact that the person was temporarily incapacitated by the embarrassment of the utmost nature and would willingly have relinquished his life, if only to avoid having to trouble the attendees. I, of course, didn't feel any such deep emotion and it might somehow have affected my performance, apparently, which was less than ordinary. It became obvious because the speaker was visibly distraught as if I was a hooker late for a prepaid fuck.

'Thanks for gracing us with your presence. May I know the time, please?' he asked. He had a carefully dishevelled look around him with white hair and beard probably clipped a few days ago; he seemed the type who was edging towards retirement and was surviving that by having half-a-dozen pegs of whiskey, neat, each evening, and on this particular morning, was suffering from a bad hangover.

'It is 9:23 a.m. I am sorry for being late. Bad traffic.'

'I see. Obviously, you didn't get much time to shave either.' Now, I was an ugly hooker who was late for a prepaid fuck. 'Did you also forget the training material?'

'Yes, Sir. I did,' said the ugly hooker who was late for a prepaid fuck and who had also forgotten the handcuffs.

'Please take a seat and try to manage it without disturbing the other diligent participants,' he said, with the pleasure of having scored one of his first victories evident in his smirk.

I looked at the room trying to assess the least conspicuous place to sit. There were a couple of chairs available right at the end and I decided to place myself there for what would be a series of monologues from middle-aged corporate marathoners trying to justify their life-choices in order to seduce us. I borrowed a pen and a paper from my neighbour, mostly because scribbling notes seemed to be the norm and I didn't want to invite any more attention to myself than I already had. In any case, now that I had a pen and paper in my hand, I could take up my as-of-now deceased hobby of drawing. It had always filled me with peace. I remembered the last time I drew. It was when I was anxiously waiting for my B-school entrance interview results; one particularly dull afternoon, I was so agitated that to calm myself, I had started reducing the view from the front window of my room to a two-dimensional scrap of paper. Well, not really my room because I shared it with my brother. Since the other window panes didn't present a view owing to a desert cooler intruding through them, the lone window pane showed a slanting vision of an almost empty street in front of my home. The tar was glistening in the scorching heat. There was a lone tree protruding from the almost grey park that I knew existed on the left just beyond the sight. The tree afforded little respite from the temperature to some of the stray street dogs who always chased my father's scooter. There was a street branching out on the right where there was a small school which would have an exodus of tiny tots from it any minute, it being the end of the school day. It was not entirely different a view from what it had been recently, except that I didn't belong there anymore. Even the blue walls felt abandoned and looked at me with hostility.

Back in the present, there was a round of applause signifying the end of this particular session. In my opinion, it was less a gesture towards the speaker and more an appreciation for the end of the session and the opportunity for a break it presented. Before the participants could move out, somebody, presumably the coordinator, announced that we were supposed to collect our laptops and other gizmos from the helpdesk. There was a murmur of appreciation from the crowd. Some of them had their jaws touching the floor and their tongues rolling out like wet, glistening, red carpets. They had probably never touched a laptop before and were now feeling sufficiently important, that is if the job itself hadn't come with adequate vanity. My ears heard vague speculations about the laptop models and the latest configurations available. I reckoned it best to collect my machine later so as to avoid the sight of communal orgasmic delights as some of these easily-excited juveniles collected their trophies. Instead, I decided to steal a quiet smoke downstairs while the others were busy with more important stuff.

I went back to the plant cemetery on the ground floor where a few chairs were placed in a haphazard manner around a custom-made ashtray with a long hollow leg which also acted as a waste dump. Dev was already parked there as if this was his permanent cubicle. He had also carefully chosen the chair most distant from the entrance, in an overly apparent effort to provide a disincentive to trespassers. Outside, the road traffic blared like it was being abysmally tortured.

'So how is the orientation going so far?' he asked, as I took the chair next to him.

'So far, so good. Can I borrow a cigarette from you?' I realised that I had left my pack in the apartment.

'I have a better idea. I am carrying a ready-made joint. Wanna share?' he said, mischief in his eyes.

'Well, that sure can help me get through the atrocities going on upstairs,' I couldn't help smiling. 'What time did you get up?'

'I just got into the office about ten minutes ago, felt groggy and so thought it best to clear my head before joining you guys.

Besides, I reckoned that if I slide in when the session changeover is happening, nobody would notice.' He chuckled sheepishly, and passed me the joint.

'Good idea. I actually thought you were an intern.'

'No. My situation is the same as yours. Stuck in an apartment filled with kids,' he said. 'So, I hear we will be allocated to different areas over the next few months before they decide where we fit best.'

'So I have heard, too. They haven't made it clear so far, though.' I took a drag and felt the iciness hit almost immediately. 'Any idea what project you will be doing?'

'I will be working on developing intelligence about their key competitor. Highly classified stuff. Anyway, I am down here to avoid thinking about work for the time being. What else is up? What else do you get up to besides smoking up and masturbating?'

'You make smoking up and masturbating sound like very basic things that every human being has to do', I was smiling to myself, the cannabis accentuating the mood. 'In any case, I don't masturbate. I pride myself in exercising self-control.'

'Bullshit. Either you can't get it up or you must have a girlfriend parked somewhere who frequently gifts you a blowjob.' The joint was half-finished and left a rotten smell in the air.

'As a matter of fact, I do have a girlfriend parked in Jaipur. However, she is as likely to give me a blowjob as allowing a camera to be installed up her legs.' As I said it, I started to visualise it and almost fell off my chair with laughter.

'Let's join those two over there. They seem to be having quite some fun. Maybe us oldies can also get some.' The artificially hoarse voice developed by years of chain-smoking came at us from the entrance. We were momentarily frozen like a couple of naked adolescents who could not hide their erections in front of their own mothers. Two middle-aged guys were walking towards us dragging their authority behind them.

'Shit, that's David, the country head with his sidekick, Dheen. We have got to get rid of the joint.' Dev stood up, visibly hassled. He was trying to figure out where to extinguish the joint and after a painfully slow moment, he saw the ashtray on the table and used it vigorously.

'Let's light a cigarette. That will help take care of the smell,' I said. Dev took out two cigarettes and passed one over to me. I lit it and took couple of quick puffs so as to kill the marijuana smell lingering in the air. Then, the two men were onto us.

'How are you doing, boys?' said David. He sported a short crop, showing off his male-pattern baldness and his face was double, or maybe triple-layered with the fattest and whitest human skin I had seen. His hunched back and protruding gut made him look sixty, although he probably was in his late forties. When my augmented imagination pictured him as a Caucasian frequenting the Mumbai dance-bars, I had to exercise a Herculean self-control to keep a straight face.

'Hope we are not disturbing you,' he continued. This was more a statement than a question, with a 'dare disagree here' attached to it.

'Not at all. We were just getting through with our morning ritual here. My name is Dev Das. I am the new hire from Delhi University.' In an effort to avoid eye contact, he was trying to smoke, but for some reason wasn't able to.

'Hi, I am Achet. You might remember me from the interns group of the last year. I have just joined today,' I said.

'Of course, we remember you, Achet. Your presentation was fantastic. Nice to have you join us,' said Dheen. He had a nice double chin and was one of those people who smoked without inhaling at all. He probably looked at smoking as a chance to kiss some more of that flabby ass attached as an oversized accessory to the rear of David. He then asked, 'Achet? What kind of a name is that?'

'I was very absent-minded as a kid and my mother had a peculiar sense of humour,' I replied. I was used to this question. While I myself had never bothered to find out the genesis of my name, I had developed this disarming response via trial and error. As usual, it got the smiles.

'Are you missing a light?' asked David, pointing to Dev's cigarette and I realised why he wasn't able to smoke.

Dev was still oblivious of the fact that his cigarette wasn't lit when he answered, 'No, I am fine, thanks.' He continued his futile attempts at extracting some smoke out of an as-yet-dead stick.

After a somewhat awkward silence, Dheen made an attempt at small talk, 'So how is your training going on?'

'It is going on nicely. We had a nice first session just now. They are distributing the laptops and other accessories at the moment. It will be interesting to see how many of us go back and check out porn on the Internet tonight,' I replied, chuckling. 'I would actually pay to get a hand on that piece of statistic.'

There were further smiles all around except Dev who was beside himself with impossibly loud laughter punctuated by many snorts. By the time he finally managed to regain control, the rest of us were staring at him; me with amusement, the others with shock. I chipped in with, 'He is a little high-strung,' which got assenting murmurs.

'Can I borrow a light?' Dev had, by now, realised what he was lacking; David offered him a lighter and asked him to keep it as he got up to leave, Dheen close behind him. 'Catch you next time around.'

When they were sufficiently out of earshot, we both burst out laughing, partly because we saw the funny side of it and partly because we also realised how silly we were to land ourselves in such a career-threatening situation. 'Man, we could have lost our jobs right here, right now. Fucking hell,' said Dev while lighting his cigarette. Moments later, we burst out laughing again because he had lit it from the wrong end.

We had smoked ourselves silly and loved every moment of it. We could almost sniff the end of our career and the fact that we had escaped filled us with a sense of invincibility. A rather false and transient feeling but it felt good nonetheless. To celebrate this small sense of victory, we decided to visit a nearby 'family bar and restaurant' and indulged ourselves with a few rounds of gin and whiskey each. By the time we got back, we had missed, rather escaped, two entire sessions and the lunch-hour was on. I picked up my plate and filled it with an assortment of visibly bland food. In an effort to blend in with the group inconspicuously, I joined a table with the least number of people. The conversation revolved around speculation about our respective chances of being posted abroad.

'Yaar, Singapore will be the place to be in. I have heard that the nightlife there is simply amazing and the pussy very easy. I really hope I am posted there,' said a completely bald person, as I eased myself into one of the unoccupied chairs.

There was a quick round of introductions, more acquaintances added to an already overflowing and at the moment buzzed-out memory. 'What is your story? Where do you want to be posted?' somebody asked me.

'Well, to be frank, I haven't really thought about it. What are the possibilities? I am sorry, I am not completely aware of all the details.'

'You must have been sleeping when they told us about it.' I turned red with pride. He continued, 'He he. I don't blame you. Anyway, we will be rotated in different roles over the next few months before they decide what our best fit is. The roles will be across various functions and the locations would be across India, Singapore and in some rare cases, other Southeast Asian countries.'

'Hmm, that is hardly a choice. I am sure it is Singapore for me,' I commented with faux surety.

'Haha, ladies and gentlemen, make way for Prince Achet.' They all acted as if they were laughing at his joke but the way they hid their faces behind their spoons and their napkins, I could make out the silent words, 'Yeah sure, smartass.' I imagined an alternate world where they would hang the one who is honest, ridicule the one who is toeing the politically correct line and celebrate the one who is a downright liar. I was sure to prosper in such a world. Then I realised that I didn't need to imagine such a world. I just needed to open my eyes.

I was attracted to Dev's self-destructive lifestyle like a moth to the light. It wasn't just the alcohol and the weed. Those were merely conduits. I was developing an unhealthy, almost evil, disregard for work which was soon to become my unbiased outlook towards everything, including myself. It wasn't constructive but as Dev pointed out a while ago, it was addictive because it was cool. It did help that I was also lucky. Dev wasn't.

3

Welcome to the Jungle

'WE WERE REALLY impressed with the project that you did last year and if that performance is anything to go by, we will be expecting a lot from you,' Rashmi said while we were filling ourselves with stale caffeine dispensed from an automatic coffee-maker. 'So, in line with the principle of making sure that our best candidates get the maximum cultural, geographical and multi-functional exposure, we have decided to train you in Singapore, India and Malaysia respectively. I hope you are excited with this state of affairs?'

'Very much so. When do I start?' I looked at her from across the coffee table in the colourful cafeteria. Even the chairs were of different bright colours, probably initially designed for a kindergarten classroom. She was pleasurably plump and I was having difficulty keeping my eyes off her bust.

'You will do the first part of your training in Singapore, starting as soon as you can book your tickets with the travel desk. Now, I have to rush for a meeting but I will need two hours to prep you. Some of the details are already in your inbox, if you care to check. It would be good if you go through them before our meeting.' With that, she quickly disappeared from the cafeteria. For a short woman, her legs moved incredibly fast. I imagined what those legs could do in bed. I wondered if it was too early in the day to masturbate and contemplated a trip to the restroom but in the end decided against it.

I found an empty cubicle and parked myself there. As I sat waiting for my machine to start, I could hear fingers tapping away at other machines around me. I could hear voices on the telephone in the distance but they seemed too far off. I looked around for familiar faces without really expecting to find anyone. There was no surprise and I got back to waiting patiently for my machine to boot. It made the usual waking-up sounds, like as the Super Mario video game that I used to play with stolen one-rupee coins. I looked up and saw a stranger looking back at me; she quickly looked away lest I should recognise her and ask her the difficult question: 'Hows life?' I had no interest in her except maybe for the low cut of her blouse. The machine was ready now and there were quite a few e-mails in my inbox, giving instructions on what I needed to do over the course of my training. I wanted to postpone going through the e-mails and so I started by first counting them. There were seventeen e-mails in total, from three sources.

I considered embarking on an experiment to list down the number of e-mails one received on successive days and whether that would throw up any important discovery. Common sense prevailed and I had to concede that I could do a better job by generating random numbers. Next, I considered the colours of the e-mail and tried to deduce the personality of the sender. I could find only one pattern and that was in Rashmi's e-mails. All her e-mails were red and marked with an exclamation mark which meant 'Urgent'. She was likely always in a hurry. I pitied her unfortunate husband. There were probably no kids since she would have long emasculated him. She would insist on going through sex with clockwork precision, the clock moving faster with practice as she would become more and more efficient at various movements. On the brighter side, at least her husband wouldn't have to bother with foreplay. I could not find anything else to procrastinate with further and so I decided it was time that I actually started reading the mails. Slowly, surely, my fingers found the rhythm. I tried to find loopholes in as many e-mails as I could. In some cases, I replied asking for clarifications as I feigned lack of understanding of some of the jargon used. In other cases, I had to shamelessly ask the meaning of a particular sentence because I could not 'understand the grammar here'. In one particular instance, I experimented to see how far I could go and simply replied with a 'Huh?' Just when my creative juices were flowing and I was becoming more daring, all of a sudden, the whole place came alive. I worried if somehow my replies had gone to everybody but realised with relief that this was simply an organisational announcement. Still, everybody was looking excited and I wondered what could be so interesting about an organisational announcement. The more I thought of it, the more I became sure that it could only be for lack of anything better to do. I told myself that this would be a good way to kill time before the first smoke of the day.

The announcement was over. Somebody had decided to quit his job and somebody else had agreed to double-hat for some time before a suitable replacement could be found. Against common expectations, however, the double-hatter would not be getting double wages. Speculation abounded. Different people expounded upon different theories and for a moment I felt I was in the middle of a soap opera. I did what I had to. I escaped and got into the lift, heading for the ground floor. I was not alone. On the third floor, others got into the lift. It seemed like it was going to be crowded. I didn't particularly like crowds. On my first smoke-break of the day, I had always preferred to do it quietly and alone, and in a decent clearing where I could walk to and fro. This was very important for me on this particular day as I adjusted to the mundane day that was to follow and the mediocre value that I would be adding to the world on that day. But, I said to myself that a break in a crowd is still better than no break. I took out my box and extracted a stick out of it. I lit it with the help of a lighter and watched it simmer.

I inhaled my first smoke deeply as if I couldn't get enough of it. I tried to keep it inside for as long as possible before slowly exhaling. I started to feel good. I thought about the previous night and recalled the conversation with Dev. I was inspired and a line flashed through my mind: smoking is an inspiring moment of self-realisation. I was proud of how I could trivialise almost everything. I took a couple of puffs more and I could almost feel the weak brain cells dying, replaced with fresh ones as the blood rushed to my forehead. The stick was now three-quarters burnt out. As always, I wanted to get as many puffs as I possibly could out of the remaining bit. A sort of tussle started between me and fire. I felt triumphant as I sneaked two full and one-half puffs. Another epiphany. If I could cheat as much out of my life as I was able to cheat from a cigarette, I could have been someone else, someone important. The break was over. I was ready to survive the day mindlessly, until the next break, of course.

By the time, I was done with the e-mailing, a euphemism for writing back and forth until somebody decides to give in and thus get the work done, not unlike the game 'who blinks first,' it was lunch hour. I dreaded eating in the colourful cafeteria but I was hungry. The food, at least on paper, was pretty much a replica of the menu at any respectable dhaba but the taste was 'corporatised' – just like the people. I wondered if 'corporatised' was even a word but it seemed to make the right connect in my mind. I was sure the people I saw in office were no different from a random cross-section of people on the streets. However, in an office they behaved differently. The very act of observation on my part caused upheaval. It was likely that even the spices added to the food felt different and acted differently as they hit the taste buds. They tried hard to make an impression and lost the essence somewhere in the process. I concluded that even if it was not a word, 'corporatised' ought to be drafted into the English language. I ate as much as possible, till my sensory buds started threatening to kill my appetite permanently. I followed the food with a cup of coffee, thinking that if I combined two utterly bland things, something worthwhile might turn up. But no such luck, and I had to resort to my tried and tested fall-back option. So I went down for another cigarette. I considered the ashtray which was filled with something resembling urine. In the morning, it was clear water and now it was a glorious gold, owing to the mass deposition of ash and stubbed filters. If smoking was an inspiring moment of self-realisation, then clearly these were the remains of that self-realisation. I reckoned that this shade was a better gold than could be obtained by combining the urine samples of an infinitely large number of people. I pondered over the possibility of somebody conducting that experiment over the course of human history and concluded that the odds were highly favourable. I fed that monstrous liquid some of my coffee with a spoon to see if it liked it and if it would reward me with a shade never seen before. It promptly turned brown and looked dead.

When I came back, I had another dozen or so e-mails, all looking red and ominous. One of the e-mails mentioned a rooftop party in the evening in the new hires' honour, free booze being the main attraction. The travel desk called me to collect my tickets to Singapore, booked for the day after, which I promptly did. Not knowing what to do with my spare time, I went to the cafeteria and poured myself yet another cup of coffee. I was now entirely sure that the popularity of coffee in offices was a factor of extreme boredom and had nothing to do with any of the stimulatory effects associated with caffeine. An 'all important' quintessential corporate bragging conversation was ensuing around the coffee dispenser between Dev and another guy while a pretty girl stood there ready to be impressed. I joined them silently.

'…And what about Zidane's kick, man, that was sheer class. I could have watched that over and over.' Dev was animatedly acting out the kick, either because the words weren't enough to describe it or because he had low opinion of his audience' listening and comprehension skills.

'Well, if it weren't for the pass, he wouldn't have been able to score, though.' The other person was doing his best to find loopholes in Dev's statement in order to prove his (superior) love and knowledge of the game. I started observing the girl and busied myself in doing a character assessment on her. She must have been around twenty-five years old and probably a couple of years in this job, this being her first job. She looked modern with a very short, boyish haircut and seemed to take good care of her appearance. Her skin was smooth and unmarked. The dark regions under her eyes suggested insomnia or a possible recent break-up. She still seemed to be confused about who she was and who she wanted to be. One thing was clear: just like me, she was here purely to kill time. Admittedly, however, she had the added benefit of being entertained in the process with this peacock dance going on around her.

'Hi, Achet. Do you follow soccer?' Dev's question not only brought me out of my reverie but also focused the group's attention on me. It was evident from the awkward looks all around that I must have been subconsciously staring at the girl. I tried to recover, 'No, I don't. I am more into movies and books.'

'Is that so? Which was the last book you read?' The sceptical question from the girl was almost expected.

'I am currently reading a book which contains articles on the all-time ten best philosophers in the world, written by the current top ten philosophers in the world.' I had briefly glanced at this book at the bookstore at Jaipur airport and had immediately discarded it as beneath me. I reckoned that its readers would likely be those who needed to brag about what they read. 'It isn't a bad read.'

'Aha! Philosophical, are we? So, do you believe in God?' Not surprisingly, the unnamed guy wanted a part of the action as he tried to strip me of my legitimate right to lie harmlessly, without being categorised by cynics or be tried by the sceptics.

'Just to clarify, I also read Harry Potter. In fact, I love Harry Potter. As for God, it's a relative term and lends itself to different meanings to different persons. I am not sure what it means to you. In any case, I am not sure whether I believe in God. I think the word is agnostic.'

'Eggnostic? What is that?'

'Exactly what I said – somebody who isn't sure,' I said. 'You may want to just stick with Zidane. I hear a lot of people consider him to be God.'

That was the first casualty of the group as apparently, as soon as it became confrontational, he didn't want any part of it. He left unceremoniously, mumbling something about having to do a lot of work.

'Do you even know who he was?' asked Dev, making no effort to hide his amusement.

'Not really. Who was he?'

'Mate, one of us, and maybe you might end up reporting to him. I wonder whether you will want to develop a belief in God then and ask Him to help you when our man screws your happiness.' He smiled, 'By the way, meet Bala. She is two years our senior.'

'Hey, Bala. Nice to meet you. I'm Achet.' I surprised myself with the pleasantry. 'Are you guys sticking around for the evening party or will you be coming back later?'

'There is no point in going home and coming back, the traffic will eat us alive. In any case, they will open the bar in about half-an-hour, much before the party is supposed to start. We might as well make the most of the free booze.' A seasoned Bala offered practical advice. Her words ran into each other and her voice carried with it a kind of vulnerability I associated with a girl who had been kidnapped in her teens by a psychopathic serial rapist and only recently released. 'We can kill time by smoking downstairs.'

Dev suggested in an ever- so-opportunistic manner, 'I suggest we go up to the rooftop and kill time there. That way, we can lay our hands on the liquor as soon as it arrives.'

We had spent close to two hours drinking before the first of the others joined us. I was already a bit intoxicated and the company of a beautiful lady next to me wasn't really helping me in staying none too steady. I was almost sure that I had managed a hard-on some time ago. Now, the liquor had taken over but I was still horny as hell. I tried to recall who it was who had said that one can't manage two types of intoxication at the same time. I excused myself for a minute and took a walk along the roof-edge which had protective railings. This was easily the tallest building by comparison in this neighbourhood and stood out like a giant penis attached to a skinny lad. To my front was the narrow one-way street filled with vehicles – cars, autorickshaws and two-wheelers. They were communicating with each other with varying intensities of headlights and piercing shrieks of horns. On the other side of the street were two small shops; more like holes in the wall. One of them was a tea-stall specialising in *vada-pao* and the other a '*paan-beedi*' shop of which I would become a frequent customer. There were a few men trying to beat each other to get an autorickshaw to head back to the comfort of their homes after a hard day's work. There was a dog determined to haggle with the tea-stall owner till it received a loaf of bread. All this while, the traffic moved doggedly towards something precious almost like a mob marching to the Holy Land. I could smell the admix of hope and despair in the air. There was a stench, accumulated over days of living in the same clothes, coming from the beggar on the street who was no doubt worrying about his next meal. A sensuous aroma sneaked out of an autorickshaw carrying two lovers infatuated with each other as only happens in the first few days of any affair. An incense of anger was emanating from a scooter – probably a bad day at office, while a faint trace of despair escaped from the old, wrinkled lady selling potatoes and onions on her cartwheel, as she tried to get rid of her stock. They were all preoccupied with something, however hollow or conceited. I felt their collective gaze at me. They were whispering to each other in a language I didn't understand; whispering and gossiping about the drifter that I was, a drifter with no purpose and one who horrifyingly wasn't seeking any either.

But there was something else too that separated them from me. They belonged here. They would live and die each day here and they knew that their children would also do the same, as had their parents. I felt insanely jealous of them all.

Presently, I moved back to the group as somebody took the mike. Bala pointed him out as Vijay Singhal, the executive director in the company, pretty high up in the food-chain as also apparently morally challenged. She related stories of him turning up drunk at her doorstep and giving her a tough time.

'Ladies and gentleman, I would like to welcome all the new members of our company…' Vijay began.

'He seems to be quite drunk already. We might have some entertainment as he hits upon the girls around here,' Bala said, 'I just hope he doesn't hit upon me.'

'Now, as is customary, we will call upon each and every one of you to come on stage to tell us about yourself, and then identify one person from the opposite sex for whom you will need to perform something…'

'Oh no! I had prepared a long list of 'fun facts' about myself just for this occasion. Somebody forgot to inform me about the change of plans,' Dev said. His brand of wit was lost on the gathering. He had an almost empty glass in one hand and a cigarette in the other. Closer inspection revealed it to be a joint rather than a cigarette.

'Now that the rules are clear, I will lead by example. My name is Vijay Singhal. I have been with the company for thirteen years and am the Executive Director of this company. The person that I want to perform for is Ms Bala. I want to recite one of my poems which I think, suits her very well. Here is how it goes.' He cleared his throat and began singing…in Hindi.

Aapka chehra (Your face)
Aapki aankhe (Your eyes)
Yaad dilaye mujhe (Reminds me of)
Meri jawani (My youth)

I kept a straight face but Dev's face could not conceal his inner struggle as he tried to control the irresistible urge to laugh out loud. Bala simply stood there looking furious.

Aapki zulfe (Your hair)
Aapka badan (Your body)
Jala ke rakhde (Sets on fire)
Mera tan-man (My body and soul)

Before he could say more, David intervened and tried to put a humorous twist to Vijay's ditty, but this too fell flat. Some of the people were looking downright scandalised with the ramblings of this dirty old man. Bala excused herself to go to the restroom. The only smiling face was that of Dev. His smile soon faded as the DJ took over, inviting people onto the dance floor. I joined in, as did many others; I carried a glass of drink with me. Dev was throwing his arms and legs around in his strange version of a dance. A little later, I realised that my glass was missing. When I looked around for it, I noticed one foreign intern, Maria, holding her hand out with an incredulous look. Her hand was bleeding and on that white skin, it looked ghastly. We took her to the side and asked her what happened. She said in a drunk German accent, 'A glass came falling from the skies and hit my arm.' She started to sob.

I muttered to myself sarcastically, 'Oh the vagaries of this world. My glass is missing and here she is delivered one from heavens.' Everybody looked at me and I slowly made the connection, 'Oh crap! That was the last of the gin left in the house!'

Soon, another drunk and distinguished gentleman was by her side and insisted on taking her to the local hospital. But she refused, almost hysterically. 'It's just a small cut. Please, it's alright. I will manage.' However, he persisted in his demands. Something came over Bala and she said that she will take care of Maria as the fellow looked disappointed. That cut the night short as we were asked to leave. We left with a rather premature ejaculation type of feeling.

I had the sense to pick up my laptop bag before I hailed an autorickshaw. At a traffic light, I heard my name being called out and spotted Bala in the car next to the rickshaw. Maria was seated next to her and was talking to somebody on her cellphone.

Bala was gesturing that I get rid of the rickshaw and to take a ride with her. I promptly accepted her offer; nothing like an air-conditioned car in that humid environment.

'Who is Maria talking to?' I asked Bala and received a curt reply. 'The one who wanted to take her to the hospital. What do you think?'

'What's going on around here? What is the missing layer?'

'You thought that Singhal was the only dirty old man in the office? Well, this guy is even worse.' Her driving was a little erratic and too fast for my comfort. I was starting to feel dizzy with the movement and the alcohol, 'These are extremely sleazy bastards. Somebody should cut off their balls and hang it at the Gateway of India.' An old man crossing the street suddenly displayed the agility of an Olympian gymnast as he jumped out of the way before Bala could squash him.

'What have they done? I mean, getting drunk at a party and reciting a stupid little poem can't be all. Is that all?' I prodded her for some juicy news as I gripped the hand-rail with one hand and the side of the front seat with the other.

'You are damn right it isn't. You know what this guy is talking to Maria about? He is giving her an emotional rant that she should have gone with him, asking what he did to deserve such a cold shoulder etc, etc. I mean he is a married bugger, for god's sake. Poor Maria didn't know that to begin with. She was just fascinated with India and thought of him as a really good person to show her around. About a week back, he almost raped her.' The car swerved to avoid the oncoming traffic from the right and Bala rolled down her window and shouted at them, 'Motherfuckers, did you leave your eyes behind along with your brains?' Thankfully, they were out of earshot. We had just jumped a traffic light. In their place, I would have replied, 'Yeah, but my dick is still with me. Do you want to come taste it?'

I tried my best not to think about her driving while silently telling myself that autorickshaws were much safer. They were slow and one could jump out if one had to. I didn't think I would jump, though. I had never been in an accident really and I might have stayed back just to check what it would be like. Besides, jumping out of an autorickshaw would be somewhat uncomfortable. 'That's sad. Why didn't Maria report it?'

'I did but Vijay told me to drop the charges and that it would never happen again,' Maria replied. She was finished with the call. I asked her how her cut was and she showed it to me. It was just a scratch, judging by the small band-aid that covered it. 'I was just scared seeing the blood. It's not too bad actually.'

'That's not all. These fuckers have turned up at my doorstep extremely intoxicated and you wouldn't believe the kind of lewd behaviour I have had to put up with.' Bala screeched to a stop in front of my apartment. I thanked heavens for having arrived safely. I waited for the whole upper body of the car to slide off the wheels. When that didn't happen, I gingerly opened the door, half expecting it to come off in my hand. I got off, bade the girls goodnight and walked cautiously towards the lift. My head was spinning from the liquor and the drive. I had to puke before I could finally sleep. It was a highly intoxicated deadbeat sleep.

More than anything else, I think what saved me in the end was my incompatibility with the 'new morality,' as it was explained to me later. I was able to get off the ride just before Dev smashed it all to oblivion. It was a pleasant surprise that some values were resident in me, dormant or not.

4

Living on the Edge

WHEN I WOKE up, I actually woke up in my dream. I must have been dreaming about something and my body clock was trying to stir me awake. In the confusion, my eyes complied with the body's order but the mind still kept on dreaming about whatever it was that I was dreaming. As a result, the dream spilled out from my head into the whole room. I could see colourful shapes and exquisite movement just like I normally would in a 70mm cinema theatre, but with three-dimensional effects. I had to shake my head several times before it cleared. By the time it did, I could not remember what the dream was about, which was quite disappointing because it was a rare occasion when I had dreamed something pleasant.

I told Ramesh, our manservant, to prepare breakfast for me and jumped into the shower. Ramesh surprised me with a very nice set of vegetarian sandwiches and a cup of steamy hot tea. This greatly helped me in getting my hangover within manageable limits. When I went down, I got a lift from an unknown colleague who kept talking about how he always wanted to form a rock music band but had ended up in a nine-to-five/six/seven/eight/nine job. He also unveiled his plan of starting a band with his old friends once he had made enough money. I met such people often enough and termed them 'glorious losers'. You could find them in every alternate cubicle. They thought they knew what they wanted to do but their choice of occupation screamed disagreement. Even allowing for the fact that some of them might have genuinely known what they wanted to do, it escaped me why they would simply rationalise and make up excuses about not doing it. To top it all, they actually genuinely believed that they had it all planned out and that they were just waiting for that auspicious date. In this particular case, it was by the time he had made enough money. If only I recognised some such calling in my life, I would surely do something about it. I didn't ask him if he had a particular date in mind because I was sure he had. Not surprisingly, I didn't register his name. I managed to thank him for the ride while parting company at the elevator.

I got to my assigned cubicle and stood about, vaguely unsure for some time. I felt that I needed to spend some time understanding that vague feeling while I had a cup of tea. So I did but just couldn't fathom its depths. So, I tiptoed stealthily back to the empty cubicle hoping I would feel less vague now. The shapeless feeling was still waiting for me and seized me as soon as I appeared. This time there was no escape unless I confronted it. It was only when I realised that my laptop was missing that I felt comfortable again. I debated whether I should go back to the apartment and get it. My body was ready but my mind vetoed the decision, citing laziness. It was such a brilliantly original excuse that I had no answer to it. Why, if only all the bosses in this world could accept such an excuse in as matter-of-fact fashion as I had, I could almost see a fleeting glimpse of Utopia. Eventually, I cast aside such wishful thinking and concerned myself solely with my very first problem at my very first job. To ensure thoroughness, I laid down all the options. There was the possibility that I could report the laptop as lost but discarded it. After all, it wouldn't look too good an entry in the file of a person in only his second day at office. It would look even more ridiculous when the person would miraculously find it the following day. Then, there was the possibility that I could get by the whole day without my computer and without anybody noticing it. That would be quite a challenge and would call upon all my creative reserves. The best part was that it would surely give me something to occupy my mind. I was sorely tempted to take it up but then had a brilliant brainwave to call up Ramesh and ask him to bring my laptop to office. I acted on it. Ramesh was reluctant and I had to dangle fifty rupees as incentive. He haggled for more but I held my ground. He called back shortly to convey the bad news that he could not trace it anywhere in the apartment. I tried to think about the last time I saw my laptop. I was pretty sure that I had packed it and had carried it with me while leaving last night. I figured that I must have forgotten it in Bala's car. I walked over to her cubicle to check with her.

'I am pretty sure that you didn't have your laptop on you when you jumped in my car. I thought that you might have left it in office,' she said. 'But if you want, here are my car keys and you can go down and check it for yourself.'

'You were as drunk as I was. So I would much rather take a look in the car, just in case,' I replied.

The car search was fruitless except that I found a lot of condom packs, some full and some empty, in the glove box. Exactly why I would look for a laptop in the glove-box was a mystery to me and I blamed it squarely on my perverse mind. At any other time, I would have had a hearty laugh about it and would have stored this piece of information for possible future recall. But at the moment, I was staring at the prospect of being the boy who lost his laptop within a day at office. I wasn't even sure about the cost of the laptop and was wondering how many months I would have to work without pay to be able to make up for it.

'Did you check your apartment properly?' asked Bala as she took the car keys back from me.

'Yes. Ramesh checked it and then I asked Dev to check again. It isn't there.'

'Whoa. You are in deep shit, man. You are going to be royally screwed for this.' I thought I saw her smiling but I wasn't too sure.

'Do you know what I need to do and who should I inform about this?'

'You will need to tell Ravi about it. He is the security head around here. He should be able to guide you.' Now I was positive that she was enjoying every moment of this. I didn't blame her as I would have done the same in her position and possibly more blatantly. 'But first of all, you have to be clear that you actually lost it and where exactly you lost it.'

'I think I left it in the autorickshaw when I switched to your car. That's the only plausible alternative.' I added silently, 'Who cares, anyway.' 'What is this guy Ravi like?' I asked aloud.

'I will let you find out for yourself. I wish I could be there as a fly on the wall but I am sure you will tell me everything about it later.' She was not even trying to hide her pleasure anymore and was openly sniggering. I was disgusted and went down for a smoke and to figure out how to present my case to Ravi.

'Yes, Achet. How can I help you?' Ravi said with the air of a person who had pressing demands on his time. He was really tall. Like many middle-aged, tall people, his shoulders stooped and his paunch was constantly threatening to uproot his shirt buttons. It was a wonder that his centre of gravity stayed within his body.

'Well, we have a problem here...' I started.

'Before that, where is your employee access card?' He jabbed his long finger at me.

'Here it is.' I took it out of my breast pocket and showed it to him.

'What is it doing in your pocket?' he asked.

'I am sorry I didn't understand your question.' I wondered if it should have been stapled to my face.

'Obviously you were sleeping when I conducted the session on security,' he said. 'In fact, I don't remember seeing you in my session.'

'You might have missed out on me. There were just too many people there. I am not too hard to miss.' I tried to smile and imagined his expression if he were to find out that I was drinking at the nearby pub at the time.

'Is that so? So tell me why do we provide the ribbon alongside your access card?'

I maintained silence without really knowing where this interrogation was going. Although I figured that with his line of questioning, it was not the best of times for me to break the news of the lost laptop. I told myself to be on the look-out for any possible window to slip the news in.

Satisfied with the exercise in intimidation, he answered his own question. 'So that you can wear your access card around your neck and we could identify you as a colleague.' I welcomed myself to the twenty-first century wherein a person had only two ways of identifying himself, his Gmail ID and his corporate ID.

'Oh yes. I forgot about that. I will have to be careful next time around,' I replied while secretly thinking about the time when slaves were marked with hot iron in medieval times.

'You had better be. That will be all.' Having scored his tiny victory over me, he conveniently forgot that it was me who had asked to meet him and that I hadn't really been allowed to speak much so far, except responding to the interrogation. I was sure that he had the entire list of employees pasted in his locker and he routinely struck out the names of the ones that he had successfully violated.

'Er, I need some help from you. I think I have misplaced my laptop,' I blurted out. The time to look for windows of opportunity was gone and desperate measures were called for.

'I must have misheard you. Did you say you have misplaced your laptop?' He was incredulous.

'Yes, sir. I have looked at all the places and can't find it anywhere and I have to fly tomorrow to Singapore.'

'You don't misplace something like a laptop. You misplace a cellphone or your underwear but not a laptop. It's too big and too bloody costly to be misplaced.'

'I understand, sir. But it is a fact and the sooner we come to accept it, the faster we can get on with our respective businesses.'

I had read somewhere that any new idea or bad news went through the motions of ridicule, denial, contradiction and finally acceptance. I just didn't have the patience to go through all the phases and tried my best to jump right to the end.

'What did you just say? Are you telling me how to do my job? Do you know how many times I get a report of lost access cards, files, cellphones, jackets, shoes, shoe-laces and what not? And do you know how often they always seem to find the same things in their bedrooms, in the wardrobes, in their toilets, under the table, on their desks and where not? Let me tell you the answer – almost all the time.' He was furious, 'I insist that you go back and take a look in every place you have been to since you last saw your laptop. I don't care if it is a whorehouse or a dance bar, a gutter or the underside of the Andheri flyover.'

'I have already done that.' I was beginning to worry that it may take the better part of the day to get him out of denial mode; the prospects of flying to Singapore the next day were getting dimmer.

'Have you done it yourself?'

'No. But I am pretty sure now that it is really lost.'

'Are you now? You weren't so sure to take care of it in the first place. I know people like you – the MBAs. You guys are always cocky, sure of everything in the world, aren't you? Do you know how long I had to toil before I got my first laptop?'

I wasn't sure where the conversation was heading. I briefly thought about why a security guy would need a laptop in the first place or what the MBAs had to do with it. Nonetheless, I promised him I'd take a look everywhere again and come back to him only if I was really sure.

Of course, I had no intention of doing that. I fetched Dev. We went down and had a joint each. I estimated a safe time period after which I could go back to Ravi to convince him that I had looked everywhere, and realised I had a lot of time to kill. So, I was in the mood to go for another round of drinks but Dev uncharacteristically declined. I couldn't possibly go upstairs because I was meant to be looking for the missing laptop and so, I decided to park myself at the smoking stalls to while away some more time. After five minutes or so, I went to the pub by myself and downed a couple of gins and tonic. I timed it so I'd be back by lunch-time. The news of the missing laptop seemed to have spread as was evident from the sadistic faces welcoming me with knowing smiles. I seated myself next to Rashmi so as to explain the circumstances.

'Hi, Rashmi. How has your day been so far?' I started off with small talk. I hoped her day was good, so I could spoil it for her.

'It could have been better. And you haven't really made it any easier for me.' She added, 'Ravi has just been to see me.'

'I am really sorry about that. But I have checked everywhere and I think it is as good as lost.' I told myself that it wasn't really a lie.

'Yeah, your eyes tell the story.' She mistook my bloodshot eyes for guilt. I could not believe my luck and credited it all to pot. She continued, 'Frankly, Ravi is a bit of a jerk. You should have come straight to me and then I would have handled him. He is one of those old-timers who like to prove their self-worth by picking on the juniors. Anyways, don't worry about it. I have asked them to issue a new laptop to you. Meanwhile, you will have to file a police report for the missing laptop so that we can claim insurance.'

At the mention of 'police,' I re-classified my day from eventful to exciting.

'That is great. I will go to a nearby police station right after lunch.'

But I couldn't really go to the police station right away. Rashmi asked me to stop by for a quick briefing on my training in Singapore. The quick briefing turned out to be a two-hour affair and it was only by quarter-past-four that I got to the police station.

'Babu, people lose things all the time. If I start writing reports for all of them, I could spend an eternity.' Inspector Gayaram, as announced by his badge, was quite skinny and had a neatly trimmed moustache that provided sparse shade to his upper lip while still maintaining a respectable distance from his nostrils. His face, however, was hard, and he had the jaws of a hyena; what's more, he seemed to be perpetually flexing those jaws. He must have been in his early forties. 'If somebody had stolen your computer, then it would have been different. But you are telling me that you lost it, right?'

'That is right. But, to claim insurance, I need to produce a police complaint.' I decided to run for election in my next life and change this policy, so that if anybody lost anything or so much as imagined having lost anything, he would be allowed to claim insurance. In fact, he would also be granted hardship allowance for his trauma.

'Alright babu, you sit there. I have a lot of things to do. I will attend to you in between.' He waved me aside to a corner chair where I promptly sat down and started inspecting the little room. The room was neither a square nor a circle but more of a pentagon, all the sides being of varying lengths. The biggest wall was directly behind the Inspector and there hung the pictures of Mahatma Gandhi and Jawaharlal Nehru framed in cracked glass with long-dried garlands wrapped around them. The inspector's desk was the biggest piece of furniture in the room. He sat on a revolving chair behind it which was completely at odds with the rest of the room. The chair was still covered with polythene which seemed to indicate that it was new. The desk had two unoccupied wooden chairs in front. The smallest side of the room was taken up by a large cabinet filled with dusty files. I was sure that my report would be an unwelcome addition in that cabinet. The third wall faced the inspector and contained windows which would have opened out to the heavy traffic outside if not boarded up by yellowed newspaper. The fourth wall had a bench attached to it on which I sat, while a big door made up the entire fifth side of the room. Yellow was the defining colour of the room. Even the walls were painted yellow. It wasn't just the ordinary yellow but the colour of turd when one is sick. I looked towards the roof expecting to see spider-webs and was, in fact, rewarded with the sight of a lizard, too.

'Why were you carrying something as bulky as a computer in the first place?' Inspector Gayaram asked while signing a bunch of papers bound to a file by thin red string.

'It was not really a computer. It was a laptop, a kind of a smaller version of a computer.' I tried to explain using gestures while maintaining a positive attitude. At least, he had heard of a computer.

'Are you taking me for an idiot? Of course, I know what a laptop is. Why didn't you mention it before? Why, I have seen a laptop myself when the minister came to inspect us last year.' He then said, 'Can you contact it?'

'Contact it?'

'Yeah, you know, like call it?'

'Call it?'

'Why are you repeating everything I say? Just answer the question, will you?' He glowered at me.

I kept quiet, unsure of what to say. I was beginning to believe that one out of every three questions was not supposed to be answered in the grown-up world. But I was having a difficult time figuring out which one.

He continued, exasperated with my lack of technological prowess, 'Like when you lose a cellphone, you can call it, right? Can't you call your laptop like that?'

It took an insane amount of effort for me to refrain from laughing my guts out but I somehow managed. A number of possible responses flashed through my mind like, 'I called but it went to the voicemail' or 'I called but the laptop wasn't home' but I settled for a rational response: 'No, I don't think you can call a laptop. It is just like a computer except that it is smaller. You can't call your computer, can you?'

'Are you sure about that? Nowadays, anything is possible. What about e-mail?'

'What about e-mail?' I blurted that out before I could check myself and immediately realised I'd made a mistake. This was that third question that I wasn't supposed to answer.

'Acting smart, are we? Don't think you can fool me. Tell me the truth. Have you sold it?'

'Are you kidding me? Yesterday was my first day at office and you think I will throw away a good job for a bloody laptop?'

'A good job, eh? How much are they paying you?' He eyed me with the interest of a vulture.

'Just about enough. Listen, can you just file a report and then could I go?' I was getting tired of his little game.

'You think you are the only busy man around here? I have tonnes of things to do myself,' he retaliated, then muttered, 'Alright, I will need two things, a letter from your company stating that the laptop belonged to them, relating the circumstances of your losing it, and your appointment letter along with your salary details.'

As I was walking out, a guy in plainclothes followed me and suggested that I pay five hundred rupees to have the report filed. Somehow, I didn't have much faith in the promise and walked out of there with a feeling that it was probably easier to steal something than report a theft.

I didn't want to waste time gathering all kinds of documents and so I went to another police station. Learning from my previous experience, I cooked up a story about how the autorickshaw driver ran away with my laptop just as I was buying a pack of cigarettes. This time, the officer-in-charge looked much more professional and promised to follow it up immediately but he still didn't write the report. I was quite tired by then and decided to skip office, so, I went home straight but after stopping for a couple of neat gins. A surprise was waiting for me there, delivered by a breathless Ramesh without any preamble.

'*Saab, police aayi thi* (Sir, police had come)'

'Huh? Why?'

'*Aapka laptop chori ho gaya tha, na. Unhone paan-beedi shop par pooch-tach bhi kari. Aur aapko thane bulaya hai* (Didn't your laptop get stolen? They inquired at the *paan-beedi* shop as well and have asked you to report to the station).'

My first reaction was that of admiration at the supreme efficiency of the operation. This was almost instantaneously followed by utter anxiety as if somebody had knocked out the wind with a massive punch delivered to my solar plexus. Very clearly, my cover was blown and I was in trouble. I didn't have the heart to go to the police station. So, I tried to ignore it like one would avoid household chores. I slept on the couch only to be woken up by a call which demanded that I present my ass immediately at the police station. The wall clock displayed the ungodly hour but I didn't have much of a choice. As I entered the police station, I passed a couple of women busy haggling with constables. They were prostitutes. One of them was offering to pay in kind but the constable wasn't interested. He was probably gay. Inside the cabin, the inspector was repeatedly slapping a worn-out soul without offering anything in explanation. Perhaps it was routinely expected of him to slap every worn-out soul that he could find. The perpetrator was complying respectfully, in line with Gandhian principles. I was subtly acknowledged by the beater with a nod towards a chair. The beaten gave me a longing look as if he were hoping I would shortly take his place. The brutal treatment lasted about half-an-hour, after which the inspector took his seat on the other side of the table. He mopped the blood off his hands with a dirty cloth which must have seen all kinds of blood samples.

'Mr Achet, so tell me what is going on?' inquired the inspector.

'Nothing really.' The voice surely didn't belong to me.

'Is it, now? We went searching for your laptop, you know. And it turns out that you have been lying to us. Is that what we get for serving the public – to be sent on a wild goose chase?'

'Listen, I can explain but it still may not be able to justify my lying.' I remained sincere even though I couldn't help smiling inwardly at the turn of events.

'You are damn right it wouldn't. Nothing can justify the waste of police's time. Not when there is a rape happening every minute somewhere in this country. Let me humour you but get this straight. If I don't like what I hear, you are going to jail. Do you know you can be imprisoned for up to six months for misleading the police?'

I was not listening to him anymore. I was mentally reading the headlines of next week's newspapers: an MBA in jail for six months, fired by employer, no willing employer due to serious ethical concerns, parents extremely upset, etc. I imagined the look on my parents' faces as they would hear this news and surprisingly, found it a comical situation. I wondered how such a small instance could drastically alter the rest of my life and found myself almost looking forward to it. Perhaps *this* was my calling. Whatever 'this' was.

'What happened? Cat got your tongue? Start before I lose my patience.'

I narrated my story truthfully. I had resigned myself to the fact that I would spend the night in jail. Singapore seemed a distant dream. I didn't even offer him a bribe to get out of this situation because I considered him to be incorruptible. But I need not have worried. He brought it up himself and the price tag was a whopping five thousand rupees. I paid it without any negotiation. I made a humble request for him to at least write the report of my lost laptop and he complied. He even bought me a cup of tea and dropped me home on his routine round of the area. It was 3 a.m. in the morning by the time I made it back to the apartment.

This was the second instance which reinforced my fatal belief that I could get away with anything. I had subconsciously made up my mind to continue to push the envelope to see how much farther I could go in my frivolous pursuits. To my surprise, I found that there were no boundaries as long as I was comfortable with the fact that by doing what I was doing, I was also moving away from myself.

◆

5

Alice in Wonderland

Late next day, midnight in fact, I climbed aboard the airplane. It took me about two-and-a-half hours to cover fifty meters or so, as there were many bottlenecks from check-in to security-check to boarding. I was sure that the queue to hell would be faster, if not shorter. I was one of the privileged few to be travelling business class but that didn't really feel like a privilege, up until now. I was welcomed with a glass of champagne as I made myself comfortable under a blanket in the oversized chair. My initial plan was to sleep during the flight since I was to report at the office as soon as I landed. The plan, however, changed as I was introduced to the concept of free liquor and the in-flight entertainment system. I asked for the drinks menu, spotted a drink called Gin Fizz and ordered it. The stewardess seemed very happy to serve it to me. It wasn't everyday that somebody ordered a Gin Fizz on-board. To my surprise, it was actually served in a wide-mouthed conical glass with little tropical umbrellas and I devoured it. It was a five-and-a-half-hour flight and I set myself the goal of trying each and every cocktail drink on the menu. With each new drink ordered, the stewardess's enthusiasm waned. Very soon, I was required to press my buzzer multiple times before she could be bothered to attend to me. Thankfully, the seat next to me was empty but something told me that even a fellow passenger's scorn would not deter me. When I exhausted the cocktails, I moved to the wine list, while simultaneously thinking of new and improved ways of irritating the staff. When the stewardess served the wine, I brought all my acting skills to the fore and proceeded to display what I thought was the perfect way to taste a wine. I swirled it in the glass and smelled the invisible aroma before tasting it in an overly-long process. Randomly, I made faces at some wines while nodding my head in appreciation of others. All the while, I watched two movies and I was disappointed when the landing announcement was made in the middle of the third movie. When I landed, my mouth was dry with the saliva sucked out by the alcohol overdose. My eyes were blank and blinking, as if in a futile bid to transition from the enticing in-flight world to the unavoidable real life. When I bade goodbye to the stewardess, she wittily remarked, 'Oh you are leaving. I thought you lived here.' Despite all that, I considered it to be an uneventful flight.

The first day in Singapore, however, was quite an experience. Even in my semi-zombie state, I could make out how organised and clean the city was. As I peered out of the window of the cab, both the greenery and the gloom hit me squarely. The city was beautifully ornamented in green but it was the same shade everywhere, like the colour originated from within a glasshouse. I half-expected that if I threw a stone really high up in the air, it would break an invisible glass ceiling. I turned my attention to the road which seemed extremely narrow but still contained four lanes. It looked like the streets back home except that the traffic was zipping at three-digit speeds. As far as I could tell, everybody stopped at red traffic lights and nobody broke the speed limit. Everybody seemed patient and there was no honking. I eerily recalled the world of George Orwell's *1984* and immediately decided to test this hypothesis by reading the newspaper. Surely, if the media was free, then it really was an open state as it claimed. The front news was about a twnty-four-year-old guy who was caught smuggling marijuana into the country. Apparently, he carried it in his blood. I read it again, then understood that he had smoked a joint while in Malaysia and when he returned to Singapore, he had some traces still left in his blood. Technically, it was smuggling drugs into the country which was punishable by death. In this special case, he was going to spend just six months in the jail. The newspaper didn't contain anything worthwhile, except an extensive coverage of the English Premiership League. There was no reporting on authentic local or global issues. My hypothesis seemed to be true. It was like a toy-state one could get to own and run. I had already condemned the city but I promised myself to be open-minded.

The office in Singapore was spread over eleven vast floors of a seventy-storeyed building which was located in a prime commercial area. It was quite a nightmare to find the way from where the cab dropped me. I entered the complex and found myself in the middle of a great hall which contained a series of shops on either side while the entire open area was occupied by a make-shift consumer fair. I stopped a person for directions but he wasn't helpful. Instead, he proceeded to try to sell me a set of various shades of lipstick at what he claimed to be a bargain.

He was disappointed when I explained that I didn't use lipstick. As a last resort, he suggested that I should. I was approached in a similar manner by multiple salesmen. There was a massive promotional-drive going on for a gym which had recently opened. No less than three 'fitness trainers' intercepted me independently as I travelled a few yards to the escalator. They pointed out the need for me to put on weight and how they could help me do that. It took me quite a while to negotiate my way through that jungle. I would learn soon enough that it was called a 'shopping mall' and that there were people in this world who could spend their entire day in them, proudly claiming themselves 'mall-rats'. The escalator took me to the office lobby and lifts. I pressed the button for the fortieth floor.

The receptionist was hiding behind an inch of make-up and looked at me suspiciously as I knocked on the glass door. She jerked her head in a questioning manner but I couldn't answer her because of the soundproof glass. I shrugged my shoulders and gestured that I needed to come in, if the knock itself didn't explain my intentions. She mouthed the word 'why' and I simply lost it. I found the situation quite hilarious. I recalled all the preparatory notes I had received but I couldn't remember any requirement of a basic familiarity with sign language. Just when I considered showing her the middle finger to see if she understood that, she finally relented and opened the door. I explained my circumstances for the good part of ten minutes. I was eventually put through to my project manager who sat on the forty-first floor. A team meeting was hastily convened to introduce me. I registered none of the names but I was impressed by their dressing sense; they had made the collective mistake of dressing up for a nightclub and arriving at the office. Some of them looked like whores and probably moonlighted as them, too. After the introduction, I was briefed on my project, which was to assist in updating a whole lot of Excel files with numbers generated by a whole lot of people. My project manager called it Spreadsheet Modelling. The person whom I would be assisting later called it glorified Excel jugglery.

The rest of the day was filled with prolonged and brutally stuffy meetings filled with mass intellectual masturbation. Most of the participants in these meetings were faceless and their voices came from the other side of the ocean. Some debated what seemingly was equal in importance to matters of life and death while others sounded clueless. I belonged to the latter group. I was expected to be a part of the discussion and to make an impression but I manufactured private reasons not to do so. Such excuses included, among others, that the matter was beyond my pay-grade or not directly relevant to me. In dire cases, I had to play my trump card: that the discussion was utter rubbish. In any case, I was obliged to sit through it just in case somebody indulged in far-fetched fantasies which necessitated my unassuming participation. I didn't think the human race had ever faced any bigger challenge in the evolutionary years than to survive such inhuman atrocities. I spent the majority of the time keeping quiet and silently thought of ways to stay awake and yet be in touch with my inner self. I would come to master such ways over the course of the next few months. One of my favourite rites was when I didn't like a particular participant and thought that his questions were not only frivolous but didn't even deserve an answer. In such cases, I would respond by side-stepping, dancing all around and on top of the question but never really answering it. I would pull out all the jargon from my reserves, mix in a few 'words of the day' from the Merriam-Webster e-mail subscription whose meaning and usage I couldn't be bothered with, and throw his rhetoric back at him by finishing my 'response' with a question posed directly back. Such intensive exercises gave me utmost fulfilment. I would count all such instances over cumulative meetings, and I would let that person off the hook only when the count reached twenty-three. I reckoned that any further exposure could potentially lead to permanent brain damage in the person. In rare cases, if I started to dream about such exchanges even before reaching the count of twenty-three, I would cease.

At the close of business, I moved to the apartment where I was to stay for a month, along with the other trainees. I hadn't slept in forty-eight hours. So, I tried unsuccessfully to sleep on the couch itself but was disturbed by my new roommate. His name was Arjuna. He was originally from Sri Lanka but had migrated to Australia at a very young age, which explained his heavy Australian accent. He was more black than brown, was built like a tank and his fitted shirt barely managed to contain his bulging biceps. His hair was clipped short, on the brink of baldness. A high but narrow forehead sat above a couple of exquisitely shaped eyebrows, under which were the longest (male) eyelashes I had laid my eyes on. When he blinked, they acted like heavy curtains; when his eyes were open, they accentuated the melancholy within. His eyes were small but they gave the impression of being large. He had an excitable childlike air around him.

'So how do you find Singapore so far, mate?' he asked me.

'I have hardly seen much of it.'

'Well, I have been here less than a week myself. But don't you worry, mate. I have got the entire weekend planned out. I have figured out all the hot and happening places around here. If you are looking for a night of debauchery, I am the man.' That was helpful. I wouldn't have to seek out a pimp anymore.

'It's 9 p.m. now. Are you sure the places will be open till late?'

'This is Singapore, mate. As long as you have eaten before eleven, you are doing well. The nightlife starts only around midnight. You wanna join me for dinner and then we can head out for some pussy-hunting.'

'Well, I haven't slept in a long time but I reckon I could make up for it during the rest of the weekend.'

'That's the spirit. I know a nice little Mexican restaurant where we can start. Let me grab a shower first. This fucking weather makes me sweat buckets.'

He came out in a dazzling striped shirt unbuttoned down to show the top of his curly chest hair; on his feet were equally loud, pointy, snake-skin shoes.

'You not ready yet?'

'Huh? I am very much ready.'

'You've got to be joking. Even I wouldn't want to be standing next to you, forget the girls.' He threw up his hands.

'What do you reckon I should wear? I'm sorry. In India, I used to roam around just like this.'

'Well, you are not in India now, are you? Show me your wardrobe.'

After a quick look into my suitcase, he was not very impressed. 'We will need to find you some clothes so that you can fit into civilisation,' he announced with an authority which did not encourage any questions. Half-an-hour later and with a wallet lighter by $323, I was transformed into a thinner version of Arjuna. Although I refused to wear pointy shoes and insisted on folding up my jeans, much to his dismay.

When we arrived at Café Iguana, a busy place by the riverside, we were ushered to a small table in a corner. We were lucky to get a table right away. In fact, it was the last empty table. The queue was now starting to reach the seating counter. The place itself was quite small consisting of only a bar in the open view, with the kitchen probably at the back and out of sight. It, however, was extended out to the river by adding additional tables and chairs, as seemed to be the common practice. Having ordered a couple of Coronas and some nachos, we settled down.

'Mate, it is best if we agree on some ground rules since we are going to be sharing the same apartment for some time,' Arjuna said as I scanned the menu for something familiar sounding. 'Do you have any concerns or specific idiosyncrasies that I should know about?'

'Nothing too important. Just don't barge into my room unannounced.' I almost added that it would be even better if you could sleep outside, if possible.

'Fair enough. Likewise. Also, I am a very hygienic guy. I like to come home to a clean place. That would mean we wash our dishes regularly, no dirty underwear unattended in the washing machine, no smelly socks running amok in the drawing room and no farting without permission.' He delivered all this in a rapid-fire manner, tongue-in-cheek. I was beginning to like him and decided to spare him my cynicism.

'Haha. I thought all that was for granted.' I smiled, 'How about if the fart is soundless and odourless?'

'If you can't be caught, then you are not a thief, are you now?' He returned the smile. 'One last thing, what if one of us brings home a girl?'

'You planning to bring a lot of girls home? On the same night?'

'No, knob. I would have loved to but I am not a porn-star. Anyways, let's just say this – if either of us is bringing anybody home, then he should text the other person to go into hiding for the time being.'

'That's fine by me. Hey, can you help me order something? I can't understand the menu. I have never eaten Mexican before.'

Arjuna ordered for both of us and then proceeded to give me a detailed account of Mexican cuisine. By the time I finished eating, I knew everything that was there to know about Mexican dishes. Any more information and I could have been presenting cooking shows in Mexico.

After the dinner, two Singaporeans joined us. Kevin and Raj were working in the same team as Arjuna. They had volunteered to show us around. Their English was unique but no different from the cab driver who had picked me up at the airport. They skipped articles on a regular basis and sometimes, they skipped entire verbs or conjunctions. As a compromise, they added a word 'lah' at the end of every alternate sentence. The effect was quite bewildering, so much so that one had to use all of one's wits to follow their meaning. Later, I would try to understand the meaning of the word 'lah' and I would realise that it didn't really have a meaning but was more of a filler, to soften a sentence; it also had as many as half-a-dozen variations.

Kevin laid down the options which ranged from the usual pub-hopping to pick-up joints. We were indecisive as ever and asked him to take us where he thought we would have maximum fun. He proceeded to explain one more option. 'We go to a street full of bars, full of girls orredy. No great music or atmosphere. You buy girl a drink and she do anything you like. Foreigners love this one, lah.'

Arjuna was sufficiently bewildered and asked, 'Anything? What do you mean?'

'Can kiss her. Can grope her. Anything, lah. You like her. You take her to your apartment.'

'You mean they are hookers?'

'No. Not hookers. Just horny little girls, lah.'

Arjuna continued his interrogation, 'How horny? And how little? Hope they are not underage?'

'Dun have underage orredy. You want underage, cost more. You wanna go or no?'

We reckoned there was no harm in just trying this place and so we found ourselves in the middle of a street lined on either side with bars with darkened glass doors. There were a few girls seated outside who were dressed in colourful mini-skirts and showed off their nonexistent cleavage. Some of them whistled as we walked by. I wondered if this town still belonged to George Orwell's *1984* or if there was something more sinister to it. Kevin led us to a bar where he was welcomed by an army of girls who seemed to know him very well. The bar was semi-full. Most tables were occupied by one single male surrounded by many girls. Closer observation revealed that the majority of the customers were balding, fat, middle-aged white blokes, with some Chinese diversity thrown in. They were engaged in nefarious activities, largely led by the girls who were alternately grinding themselves against the men's crotches or kissing their necks as the clients pretended to be bored. All in all, it seemed that all the clients were regulars here, and that included Kevin and Raj as well.

We were led to a corner table and a pitcher of beer arrived shortly after. Arjuna whispered to me, 'I don't know about you, mate but I am as comfortable here as I would be if I were forced to have sex with my mother watching. If you are okay, we better move back to some fucking civilisation.'

I replied, 'Let's see what happens. I am actually intrigued. Let's stay for half-an-hour or so and then we can fuck off.'

Raj, meanwhile, was talking to the bartender who ushered him through the backdoor. About five minutes later, he turned up with five gorgeous girls. They had pigtails and they were wearing tank-tops over short tartan skirts. They looked like they could have been on their way to a school. Around the same time, the bartender brought a tray containing thirteen shots. The whole affair was extremely synchronised, almost to the point of being poetic.

'These girls look so underage, mate.' Arjuna cribbed, 'And who the hell is going to pay for the shots? I don't have that kind of cash. Fuck me! I haven't even received my first paycheck yet. From the looks of it, I might as well ask them to remit it directly to this bar.'

I whispered back, 'Chill out, mate. We didn't buy the shots and as long as you don't touch the girls, they can't force us to pay for them. But, change of plans. We need to fuck off as soon as possible or else we face the prospects of paying up. Start voicing your discomfort to Kevin, so it wouldn't be awkward when we leave. I will work on Raj.'

The girls had divided the guys among themselves with a mute understanding developed over years of working together. A couple had positioned themselves on either side of Kevin who had his arms around them. His hands were facing a problem of plenty as they debated which breast to fondle. One had seated herself on Arjuna's lap; Arjuna looked elsewhere in a hopeless cause to pretend that he didn't know her. Raj had the fourth girl on his right arm as he leaned over to show me a photograph of an Indian girl. He asked, 'She hot?' I agreed and asked him who she was. 'My wife,' he replied proudly. 'You are thinking, I have such a sexy wife, what the hell am I here for? Be honest, eh?' I agreed once again and he proceeded to explain his reason, 'She a ball-buster, lah. Won't let me touch her often enough. Wants me to quit smoking and quit going to bars like this. But I say, to hell with her. I do what I want. She dun realise how bad I feel for doing this, but she make me do this. What can a man do, lah? Be honest, eh?' I thrust my bottom lip out and nodded to feign understanding. He turned his attention back to the girl which allowed the fifth girl to seize the opportunity as she pulled my hands around her and started caressing my neck. I looked across the table to notice Arjuna being handled the same way. Our eyes locked and we arrived at a lightning understanding, and got up to leave. To questions raised by Kevin and Raj, we both made vague excuses. Arjuna blamed his devout Christian beliefs, at which both of them rolled their eyes. I blamed it on premature ejaculation which was taken rather well. 'Happens to the best of us,' Raj said.

'We are never talking about that again. It never happened,' Arjuna declared, 'Did you really come in your pants, mate?'

'No man. But I like lying in a trivial but scandalising manner. That's my trip.'

Thereafter, we hopped across a number of forgettable places. Soon, beer was replaced with gin. By the end of the night, we found ourselves at a place called 'Insomnia' and were running solely on large tequila shots. There was a live Filipino band performing a mix of pop and rock scores while everybody else moved rhythmically, in spite of being crammed in a limited space. Arjuna said, 'Fuck! Mate, I need to sit.' I looked around to realise there was no place to sit, thought on my feet and walked up to two girls sitting by the bar, 'Excuse me? I am doing a survey on what women want. Can you tell me if you like good bodies or big dicks?' The girl right next to me looked zapped and muttered, 'What?' to which I replied, 'Either way, I am your man.' Both looked horrified and scurried away. We conveniently slid in the recently vacated chairs. Arjuna commended me on a job well done and struck up a conversation with a girl sitting across from him. I felt bored and busied myself with a hypothetical question on whether I could get a blow job if I sat there long enough without doing anything. I speculated that everything in this world had some likelihood, however marginal, of happening. I just needed to be patient, for it could take a few centuries. Somebody from the group next to me forced yet another shot into my hand, mistaking me for a friend. An automatic reflex action led to the drink being deposited in my innards. An immediate dizziness followed and I had a strong urge to throw up. I came out of the place and walked another ten minutes or so, mostly in circles, and found myself inside a toilet.

I was having difficulty staying on my feet and so I sprawled on the floor. I grabbed the commode with both my arms and threw up vigorously. After momentary indecision, I decided to catch a wink in the same position but that delay proved too costly. My insides were still trying to get rid of the foreign spirit and they had decided to try out the other exit. Somehow, I managed to get up, unbutton my jeans and sit on the pot just in time for what clearly felt like the biggest and noisiest offload of my life. Sleep followed soon thereafter.

Arjuna brought with him a welcome, almost childlike, breath of freshness. He reined me in. If I were with Dev that night, I was sure to have jumped headlong into my experimentation with stretching moral boundaries. As I would find out later, Arjuna's values were fairly different from mine but he was crystal clear on what was allowed and what wasn't.

6

The Terrorist

'How you feeling now?' asked a girl who was bending over me. It was noon and I was sprawled on the couch in front of a muted TV.

'Okay.' After a moment's hesitation, I added, 'How do I know you?'

'Don't worry. She wouldn't have slept with you even if you were on your best fucking behaviour last night,' Arjuna replied as he came out in his shorts and T-shirt. 'By the way, you did me proud last night, mate.'

'Did I now? I suppose you got me back here before the government could deport me to India, that too, on a canoe without a life jacket?'

'Yes, I did. And you owe me your life for that. I shall take it at my leisure. We are going out for lunch. You want something?'

'No, thanks. I just had some cereal and I don't think I should be torturing my stomach any more for the time being.'

'Okay. Catch you later then.'

I used the afternoon to catch up on my personal e-mails. There was one from Dev. A lot seemed to have happened in his life in the past couple of days. His original project had been squashed and he was on his way to Singapore for a new one. He described his latest project as insubstantial and more of a ploy by the company to keep him occupied. He didn't seem to mind, though. He had also broken up with his girlfriend or vice versa, and he had followed it up with back-to-back visits to dance bars in the past two nights. Apparently, he had been missing that for a long time. I felt sorry for him because he seemed to go to great lengths in trying to make light of these events. It was almost as if he was under some obligation to convince others of his carefree and jovial lifestyle. I typed a reply but didn't send it because it reeked of sympathy. I rewrote the mail but that too, had the same outcome and so, I abandoned the attempt.

My classmates had been chatting under an email-thread titled, 'My first week in the corporate world'. Some seemed to be denouncing the ethical corporate façade; others were making fun of it in a Dilbert-like fashion. Almost all had contributed. I wondered if every generation of fresh career aspirants went through the same drill and how it was that they were so radically and readily transformed into the willing pistons and pedals that formed the base for such corporate entities. And yet, reality provided ample evidence of such a metamorphosis. An insane thought entered my mind that time was running backwards and we were all beautiful if not entirely innocent butterflies about to be transmogrified into pupae, and then eventually into caterpillars; climbing and shitting atop one-another. I wrote this premise down and promised myself I'd read it again a year later.

There was also a long note from Radha. She was my girlfriend-with-no-benefits as she refused all my sexual advances to the point that I had stopped making them. There was a standing joke between us if the chastity belt's lock had gotten jammed over the years. She wanted to save it all for marriage, which was another piece of uncomfortable topic that kept cropping up every now and then. I had been dating her for as long as I could remember. At the time of my graduation, I had, somewhat reluctantly, promised to marry her. During the last trip home, the discussion had become a little touchy as I pushed for some more parole time. 'You will always be busy with something or the other. It was your studies so far and now you want to be settled in your career, and then it will be something else. When will you ever be ready? Will you ever?' she had accused, somewhat pertinently. The reality was that I didn't think I wanted to marry her anymore. In fact, I was starting to doubt if I really wanted to marry at all. But I didn't have the courage to say that aloud. The e-mail in contention, however, completely avoided that topic and concerned itself largely with her past week and enquired about mine. I knew her well enough to know what a genuine gesture it was. She was definitely trying hard not to be another indeterminate element in my life and was being supportive as I 'embarked upon another shaky voyage'. What hit me was that I no longer cared about it; not as a lover, not as a friend, not even as a hypothetical uninvolved reader of a moving, romantic tragedy.

'Looks like someone's working hard.' Arjuna was back. He had gotten rid of the girl.

'Nah. Just surfing the Net. How was your lunch?'

'Pretty good. Hope you are not surfing porn. I hate that. So what's up?' He extended his form on the smaller couch.

'Nothing much. How was your night? Was it good?'

'It was the best lay of my whole life. These fucking Orientals! Man, they are awesome in bed. I got the best blowjob ever.'

'Spare me the details, will you? Hey, by the way, I'm sorry about last night. Normally, I can hold my drink. Hope it wasn't too much of a hassle.'

'You really don't remember, do you?'

'I remember going to sleep on the toilet floor. Was there more to it?' I raked my brains for details but none was forthcoming.

'Wow. So you had a complete blackout. I didn't know anyone still could. I thought mankind would have long since evolved from blackouts with massive alcohol consumption going on for generations. But it looks like I was wrong and how pleasantly so.'

'Will you stop the foreplay and get down to the act?'

'Well, at some point of time that night, I realised that you were missing. I thought you must have been groping some chick somewhere. Soon, the place was closing down and so I went looking for you. I looked everywhere but you had disappeared like a fucking ghost. Eventually, I found my way to the toilets. There was one particular stall which was locked from inside and I started knocking on that door. You should have seen the look on the faces of those who were looking forward to a simple quiet piss. I must have knocked for about five whole minutes before I heard life stirring inside. You must have been sleeping in there and the banging woke you up. That was the time when I was given a shower of the choicest expletives ever. You were like an unstoppable, automatic, revolving-barrel machine gun with an inexhaustible supply of cartridges. To put it mildly, you told me to stop interfering with others' business, go fuck myself and let you sleep in peace. Apparently, it was the best sleep of your life and you would sooner murder me than leave that place. Finally, you relented and opened the door. That was when I was treated to the world's strongest after-puke, after-shit perfume. It was like a fucking nuclear holocaust in there, mate. I was tempted to bottle it up and put it on e-Bay as a weapon of mass destruction. Once my nose-buds were sufficiently numbed, I realised that your pants were down to your ankle. To cut a long story short, I picked you up and walked, rather shoulder-carried you through to the cab and to the apartment. Fancy that?'

'Yeah. We should do that again.' Looking at the bewildered look on Arjuna's face, I added, 'Just messing with you, chill.'

'So, which part of India do you come from? Tell me about your family.'

'Umm. I come from a place called Jaipur. It's up in the north-west, near New Delhi. We are two brothers and of course, the accompanying parents. I am the younger one. My brother is working in the US with an Internet start-up.' I added, 'You?'

'I am the elder of two brothers. The younger one is still studying. My parents live in Melbourne. It's a nice place.'

'How did you guys end up in Melbourne? If you don't mind telling me the story.'

'Well, we are Tamils from Sri Lanka and we were being raped and murdered, back in the mid-80s. Then, on top of that, you guys sent your peace-keeping force which added to our plight. One fine day, there was a Singhalese group which came to our colony in Colombo, accompanied by some Indian soldiers. They fucking dragged the Tamils out in the street and beat them to death. Even worse, the women were taken to one side and raped before being murdered. My dad was at a hotel ten miles away at the time, he worked there as a manager. I was four and my brother was two, and my mom carried both of us as she jumped walls and dodged murderers. We had relatives in Melbourne who sponsored us and we were taken in as fucking refugees. My old man lost all his fortune and had to start all over again. He did multiple jobs as an auditor, tutor, etc. He ran evening shifts at a gas-station and late night shifts at a restaurant. I think he aged about twenty years in that time. We finally made it out, which is what counts in the end.'

'That's incredible.' I said, 'It will be an honour to meet your parents. Did you go back to Sri Lanka?'

'I haven't gone back and don't want to step in that goddamned place till they give us our due. My dad, however, keeps going back every now and then and might I add, against the family's collective advice. In fact, he will be there next month.'

'What do you mean, your dues? They can't possible return the past years. Nobody can.'

'Not to us specifically, knob. I meant deliver what is due to Tamils. We deserve a state of our own.'

'Are you serious? Do you really believe that much in this cause?' I found it incredible that somebody educated could still feel that kind of nationalistic or racial passion in this age.

'I do. Admittedly, I haven't done anything to support this cause so far, but I will when the fucking time comes,' he said, visibly distressed.

'Don't get me wrong. I have nothing against you or anybody who believes in a cause, any cause, be it a jihad or a Jaffna. I was just, you know, curious…'

'Disbelieving, that the word you looking for,' he interrupted.

'Okay. Honestly, I do feel sceptical that one can still feel such strong emotions towards one's nation or race, or any other similar intangible concept. I, for one, don't think I will be enrolling in the army if my nation is invaded or my race threatened with genocide. When 9/11 happened, I wondered for a long time about what could make a person take such an extreme measure. Is it unpardonable sins committed against their loved ones or simply a matter of expert brainwashing? Whatever the case, I envy such passion whether good or bad, purely for philosophical reasons…because I have nothing of that sort.'

'Now, it's my turn to be sceptical. Well, whatever. It's good that we are different. That way, our stay here won't be boring.' He smiled. 'Let's have a smoke and discuss more important stuff like where to get our next meal.'

We stepped out to the balcony and lit our cigarettes silently. The entire left view of the balcony was blocked by an equally tall but old building. It was clearly lacking in air-conditioning since the inhabitants had their windows open and there were fans, ceiling and table, operating in most of the rooms. Directly across but a floor below, there was a room with three young lads clad only in their boxers. They were engaged in alternately playing cards and scratching their crotch. To the right of this building but further back was a two-storeyed Chinese temple with a conical roof, currently abandoned. A busy street went about its proceedings on the extreme right, perpendicular to our building.

It was lined with lamp-shops on either side, referred to locally as light-houses. These shops were punctuated with karaoke bars with dark tinted glass entrances. I would later learn that these bars were a mellowed-down version of the ones we had visited last night and their clientele consisted of average middle-aged Chinese males trying to live out their fantasies with the bar girls.

'Mate, looking at those ugly naked idiots across, let me add another house-rule. Nobody is allowed to roam topless in the house. At all times, we need to be respectably clad.' Arjuna was clearly and disturbingly captivated by the view.

'Does your father also feel the same way?' I asked, still intrigued enough to hark back to our earlier conversation.

'How does that matter?'

'I don't want to get uncomfortably personal or anything. I am still curious about the genesis of your beliefs. It's fine if you don't want to talk about it.'

He debated before divulging, 'I think he does. Though, he doesn't talk about it. Hell, he doesn't talk at all, actually. But just growing up having to look at his resigned face each day itself was unbearable enough. It was like looking at a dead mechanical machine tirelessly working for our benefit. What did he do to deserve such a life? And I do blame Lanka for all the hardships and discrimination that we faced. So, it may have originated from that.'

'Discrimination in Oz, you mean? Racial?'

'Hell, yes. In the late eighties and early nineties, there was a lot of unrest going on among the locals against and because of a large number of immigrants, mostly Orientals and some 'curries'. The locals were worried the immigrants would take their jobs and ruin their culture. The Orientals were relatively large in number and grouped themselves together to survive but the 'curries' were fewer back then. On numerous occasions I had to eat dirt while trying to protect my younger brother, and there were situations where I had to abandon attempts at wooing a prospective girlfriend. But honestly, by the late nineties, it had all settled. Nowadays, there are still racial undercurrents and people tend not to mingle with other races but broadly, you can live in peace if you mind your business. Just like any other country, I guess. How were your younger days?'

'I was fortunate to have an average childhood. Nothing out of the ordinary. A few molestations here and there but nothing too significant so as to leave any psychological mark on me,' I smiled.

'Fortunate to have an average childhood. Where is the fortunate part?'

'Huh? You don't think that having an average childhood is fortunate?'

'Average childhood is the most likely expected scenario. That is why it is called average, knob. You are fortunate if you get a swanky, luxurious childhood. Could it be that you threw up your mental faculties as well last night,' he chuckled.

'No. You are fortunate if you had a childhood that you wouldn't want to change in hindsight. I had an average childhood by any standard, and I wouldn't have it any other way.'

'Why?'

'I just answered that.'

'Don't trivialise, you fuck. I mean why would you prefer the same childhood? What was so special about it?' Arjuna threw up his hands in exasperation.

'Exactly what I said, duh. It was special because there was nothing special about it. I am happy to have turned out the way

I have and a large part of that is because of my upbringing. If my childhood was any different, I would have been a different person and I would rather stick to the tried-and-tested me.'

'Risk-averse, eh? But it's good to know that you are a content person.'

'Hey, who said I am a content person?'

'You are talking in riddles, mate.'

'Actually, it's quite simple. I am not content but I prefer my restlessness to being content. How difficult is it to understand that?' I honestly thought it was quite straightforward.

'Whoa! That's some deep shit, bro. I can't believe you are the same person who was hugging the toilet seat last night as if it was the last thing connecting you to this planet.'

'Alright. I am sufficiently embarrassed about last night. Can we move on?'

'Only if you promise to move to a real topic.'

'Like?'

'Girls?'

'Of course.'

These were the first signs that I was talking to a potential terrorist. This was also the first time I realised that I was not unique in not being able to fit in and that almost everybody had something or the other playing at the back of their minds. The only differentiating factor in my case was the intangible aspect of my quest. On the other hand, I embarrassingly admitted to myself that perhaps I was making too much out of nothing. I was proved wrong.

7

Lust in Work

I HAD THE same 'choking dream' again. This dream has been recurring ever since I moved out of Jaipur. Every dream differed insofar as the reason for the choking was concerned, ranging from being strangled by a faceless person to being stabbed in the throat. Over time, however, I had noticed a pattern. The dream and the choking had become more and more gruesome. On this particular night, it was horrendous. In the dream, I wasn't getting any breath and I was holding my throat the way a mountaineer holds onto the rope when he has tripped over the side of the mountain. To my horror I realised that my own hands were strangling me. I tried to let go but my hands wouldn't oblige as if they had a sinister mind of their own. I ended up giving a loud shriek. It was a weird shriek that couldn't possibly be identified with my voice and was probably coming from a monster deep within. I realised that I had known about the monster's existence all along but was surprised at how conveniently I had chosen to overlook the fact. Suddenly the bedroom door flew open and I sat up. The monster had escaped through my howl. It had taken a material form and had appeared at the door. In a couple of quick steps, it came and sat beside me. The whole time, it kept talking to me in a loud devil's voice, the meaning of what it said was lost on me. I was that petrified. It grabbed hold of my shoulders and started to shake me. In between oscillations, shapes stopped running into each other, the borders materialised, indistinct became distinct, and Arjuna's concerned face loomed in front of me.

'Mate, are you alright? Can you hear me? Hello?'

My hearing had returned but my tongue wouldn't move. I could comprehend everything, clearer than ever, but I couldn't respond. I was like a conscious but heavily sedated patient on the operating table who was able to see every cut and dissection but not able to feel any pain or do anything about it.

'Are you okay?' He snapped his fingers in front of me and then in an instant that lasted an eternity, I was back.

'Yeah. Yeah. I am okay. I am okay.' The moment was passing so slowly that I could see its long but slow and graceful strides as it left while mocking me. I wanted to watch it for eternity. 'Just give me a minute.'

Arjuna probably understood it or perhaps it was sheer relief that he didn't have to go out of his way to fix me up. In any case, he walked out of the room, leaving me in peace. I spent a few hours falling in and out of sleep in the most intoxicated fashion and it was only in the afternoon that I was able to get to office. Luckily, nobody seemed to give a damn about my whereabouts and I slipped in nice and easy. I told myself to further push my luck in future and see whether I could get away with not turning up at office at all. Presently, I came down to have a smoke, having pre-arranged to meet Arjuna and Dev. They were already there.

After I did a quick introduction between them, Arjuna asked, 'How are you now?' and proceeded to explain my 'morning ritual' to Dev.

'It is not a ritual. This was the first time it has happened.'

'Mate, the way Arjuna described it, you had a fit. I have an elder cousin who has an epileptic condition and it sounded exactly like that,' Dev ventured.

'Epilepsy doesn't manifest itself this late in life. I'm sure it was just a bad dream,' I was getting irritated with this shower of concern but secretly harboured a wish that it were true. Somehow, I felt, that would justify my existence.

'Nonetheless, you don't want to risk it. My advice is to seek some medical help. You know, they actually prescribe marijuana as a relaxant. If you get the prescription, even we can get some.' I imagined him smacking his lips.

'Hang on, mate. Don't ever risk that in Singapore. Prescription or otherwise.' Arjuna offered some fatherly advice, 'In any case, you should cut down on your alcohol consumption for sure. Alcohol often triggers a fit,'

'Guys, put a stop to this. I am fine and it was just a one-off affair. And please do not mention fits and epilepsy anymore, anywhere. It has a stigma attached to it. To begin with, mine was just a bad dream. Don't read anything more in it. That's it, okay?'

'Sure.'

After that, nobody spoke much. My smoke break was effectively ruined. I was hoping for a relaxed smoke with familiar faces but it turned out to be overly stressful. The day was further ruined by my acting supervisor, who asked me to build an Excel model from scratch. Now, what did I know about spreadsheets? My exposure so far had been limited to Power-Point presentations and it was to be the first time I was asked to throw myself into miles and miles of spreadsheets. He was kind enough to tell me the objective of the model and to give me complete liberty in terms of design, specifying only that it had to be as user-friendly as possible. I was sure even God had a more detailed instruction chart with Him when He created the world; although, looking at His appallingly pathetic creation, He probably didn't follow it to the letter. I roamed around aimlessly for some time, to get myself sufficiently roused about the project so as to start work on it. It didn't work. I spotted an unattended laptop and extravagantly spent half-an-hour attempting to change its wallpaper to a carefully selected Pamela Anderson photograph. I was tempted to pick a nude picture but settled for something sexier which would give reasonable exercise to the viewer's imagination. Further, I changed the browser homepage, replacing it with a homosexual porn website which played their featured movie as soon as the page was loaded. I closed the browser and turned on the volume to the maximum and walked away. As I was walking away, the owner of the laptop came back to his seat. I felt like James Bond who had just set up explosives and was walking away, waiting for the blasts in the backdrop. As it did, everybody around got up and looked at the laptop owner with disgust and grimaced. I did, too. The victim himself was momentarily paralysed. I felt I ought to be rewarded for bringing excitement into their monotonous day but I didn't think it prudent to accept the blame for the act. In hindsight, though, I should have written an anonymous letter to them, claiming full responsibility for it and demanding a reward.

In the end, I managed to force myself to flirt with the spreadsheets. They don't call it spreadsheet for no reason. One spreadsheet alone has 16.78 million cells, spread far and wide. I generated random numbers and calculated the cubic route of googol and realised to my dismay that it could have been worked out in a better way by working out the cubic route of ten. I proceeded to numbers, more complex but larger still, and was soon bored to death. Around this point, I discovered graphs and macros and was soon captivated by them but I was nowhere close to building the desired model. I was like a child playing with individual building blocks but couldn't be bothered to put them together to match the picture on the box. I still persisted and did extensive Internet search to learn more about Excel models. I found myself in an online forum when an idea struck me. I posted an offer for the model, laying down the objective and offered five hundred dollars to whoever could deliver it the soonest. That was when Arjuna came, saying he was ready to leave for the day. I was genuinely surprised to note that it was already seven o' clock. The office was still full but Arjuna wanted to postpone late hours to the latter part of his career. I couldn't find any reason to disagree and we proceeded for steak and wine. We both agreed that it was too disturbingly romantic for just the two of us and so he invited a couple of other people as well. Some major cribbing, heightened by excess wine, ensued.

'Listen to this. I am sitting in a meeting. They are discussing why the plant cannot supply as per demand. A root-cause-analysis is done and the reason cited is that the workers did not come back after the Chinese New Year celebration. Hahaha. Can you believe that? They were probably celebrating New Year by way of a tribal dance around a bonfire in some jungle and got lost. Hahaha.' This was a Filipina with an hourglass figure and a shapely behind that could launch a thousand ships. 'The second reason provided was that the workers had all left in search of higher salary. So I say, we are searching for them and they are searching for higher salary. Hohoho.' She seemed to be singing rather than speaking. I didn't catch her name on purpose. I wanted to spare my brain the trouble of irrelevancies.

The conversation continued in similar fashion. As it happens with most such conversations, all funny events at the workplace were soon exhausted. With the empty wine bottles piling up and the night becoming darker, sex insidiously crept in.

'So guys, you have been here for what, like a week? Have you identified any birds so far?' she enquired.

'For me, it will have to be Bala,' Dev revealed without any diffidence whatsoever.

'Hahaha. There hasn't been one Indian boy who hasn't named her ever since she arrived. What is it with you all? Everybody seems to be going for the same profile.' She chuckled. 'I have heard about her but never met her. But what I have heard is quite interesting. She is quite the slut, it seems.'

'What do you mean?'

'She has slept with all the Who's Who in this company. It seems to be part of her career strategy.'

'All the better. No ties attached.' Arjuna was inadvertently dripping wine from the corner of his mouth onto his shirt. 'You know the definition of a perfect girl? She's the one who leaves right after sex. Hahaha.'

'Well, so we know what kind of girls you are into, Arjuna. Be careful what you wish for,' the Filipina reproached. 'What about you, Achet? Do you like anybody or are you into boys?'

'I like you very much,' I blurted out. Laughter ensued.

'Stop it, guys. What's wrong with it? At least, he doesn't hide behind self-made moral standards or the lack of it.' When that didn't stem the sniggering, she made another effort, 'Why, you guys don't think that I am pretty?'

That did it. There was no way any polite person would have disagreed with that. My original confession was no longer distinguishing enough and the result far too unsatisfactory for the awkwardness risked. For the rest of the night, I avoided looking at her and conversed frivolously.

In time, we parted company and arrived back at our apartment. We were joined by Dev's apartment-mate, Alex. He was born in Greece but brought up by his mother in Australia. We had a few nightcaps each while sitting around a glass table on the balcony. Across the street, the lads in boxers were playing cards still. The traffic was almost non-existent but there were quite a few drunk pedestrians on the road. Some were coming out of the karaoke bars and hailing cabs while others were still haggling with the bargirls. One guy was talking to a painted girl on the sidewalk, probably negotiating a bargain.

Dev was being philosophical and later, we would learn that it was a trait he acquired whenever he was full of alcohol. 'What do you think? Have you found anybody that you would want to grow up to be?' His question was directed to nobody in particular and nobody replied.

'It is a great place to grow up in. Plenty of chicks and hot, too.' If Dev was philosophical, Arjuna was definitely horny. 'I could do that Filipina any day.'

'Get in line, mate. And it looks like a long queue, too,' Alex ventured. 'Apparently, she has a boyfriend of over eleven years.'

'Eleven years! What is she waiting for? Old age?'

'You know how Filipinos are. They start dating when they cross puberty and often they stay with the same guy. But she is friends with some really good-looking chicks and we should hang out with her more often.'

'Is it just me, the odd one out here?' Dev was clearly feeling left out. 'Is sex all you can think of?'

'The world runs on lust,' Alex said, whimsically.

'Pardon?'

'Huh?'

'Elaborate.'

Alex grew weary. 'It's fairly easy, isn't it? Why do you want to have a good education, a good career, a fast car or a mansion?'

Dev drew a blank, not knowing where the conversation was heading. I filled in, 'To earn a name for ourselves?'

'What for?'

I tried to second-guess. 'If you are going into the existential direction, then that is not very productive.'

'No, I am not. I am as materialistic as you can get. Humour me for a bit.' Alex perched upon his chair like he was fishing for a particularly scarce species and saw one playfully sniff at the bait tied to the end of the hook.

'I don't know. You tell me.' I lit a cigarette assuming his to be one of the many mediocre theories that the young and the restless indulge themselves in. Like an automated reflex action, a couple of other cigarettes were also lit.

'Throughout history, men have sought power and fame. You and I are no different. They have done so to prove that they are stronger and more desirable. To differentiate themselves from the average Joe. They have done so, in short, to entice the best lady out there and to pass on their genes. That is lust in operation. They might not know who it is that they are going after to begin with, but the idea is always there in the back of their mind, so subconscious that they probably don't even realise that it's there.'

'So the reason Dev may want to be the CEO of this company is so he can get laid?'

'That would be a long wait, mate.' Alex smiled, 'but the reason he wants to get there is to be desired and admired by the opposite sex. A different version of lust but lust nonethesame.'

'And the reason one might want to write a book is not because one has something profound to share but because one wants to be desired?'

'Exactly.'

'I disagree,' Dev stated flatly.

'I agree.' Arjuna broke his unnaturally long silence.

'How are you so certain?' I directed my question at Dev.

'Because I believe that there is more to the world than just sex.'

Alex resumed his weary tone. 'Mate, it is not about what you believe. There are guys out there who believe that the world is perched atop a tortoise. But that's not what it is about now, is it? Expound upon your disagreement. I will keep it simple for you so you can keep up. Just give me a better reason for being a CEO.'

'Because I want to be successful in my career, want my parents to be proud of me and want my peers to respect me.'

'In other words, you are seeking differentiation?' From the looks of it, Alex was fishing for another and rarer species.

'If you have to put it that way, yes.'

'Why differentiate? So people can look at you in awe. That just proves my point. It will earn you peer respect and admiration, which will further increase your desirability for the opposite sex.'

'Achet, help me out here, dude.' Dev looked at me helplessly.

'Even the evolutionary theories say the same thing,' Alex continued.

Arjuna asked, 'What about the willingness of a soldier to die for his people?'

'Dude, you have got to decide which side you are on. Earlier, you said that you agreed with Alex,' I said.

'It is alright, Achet. Don't crucify him for having second thoughts. So Arjuna, why does a soldier put his life at risk for his country?' Alex was being quite accommodating here.

'Because he passionately loves his country.'

'Let's take one step back. Let's say that there is a well-off guy who doesn't have any economic need to join the army. Why do you think he would join the army?'

'I have already mentioned that.'

'I disagree. A person who doesn't have an overriding socio-economic need to join the army, will do so only to differentiate himself from others. To try to find one's own niche. Some find it in writing a novel, others in a high-flying career, and yet others in eccentricity. The end objective is the same – somehow to distinguish oneself. And to what avail? Only to improve one's lay potential.'

'What about the person who joins the army because that is the only way for him to earn a livelihood?'

'You disappoint me, mate. That is exceedingly simple. He would join the army so that he would have a job and even an idiot knows that a person with a job has better potential than a person without a job.'

'What about people like Gandhi?' I asked.

'You mean why would Gandhi do what he did? Well, here we are entering into uncharted grounds. You can explain Gandhi's motives as one to prove his manhood to all and sundry. But there is a possibility that he was driven by superior motives. All I am saying is that by and large, the world runs on lust, not on love, but lust.'

'I continue to disagree.' Dev repeated which was further reinforced by Arjuna, who said, 'I have my own doubts.'

At Alex's questioning glance, I responded with 'I don't know.'

'What do you mean, you don't know. You have heard all the arguments. You should have a point of view by now.'

'Why?'

'Why, what?'

'Why do I need to have a point of view? I can continue to be unsure, can't I?'

Alex said 'If you sit on the fence, eventually you wouldn't belong or amount to anything.'

'How can you be so sure?' I was a tad irritated with my freedom of thought being thus taken away.

'What am I if I don't perceive? Nothing.'

'If your logic is true, nobody is anything except a vehicle to pass on the human gene, anyway.'

'Whatever.'

While Arjuna brought with him a childlike innocence, Alex added the much needed rational argument in the mix. His ability to pick up anything and strip it down to the basic essentials was admirable. By doing so, he made me feel small and irrelevant. While it may sound emasculating, the reality was that he put me back in my place with logic that was hard to negate.

8

Self-destruction

It was my medical check-up day. Apparently, the Singapore government could not allow one to work here unless one was certified healthy. The doctor was shocked at seeing somebody as underweight as me. It was evident when she asked me if I had been sick recently, to which I replied in the negative. She proceeded to poke and needle me to her satisfaction. When she was done, she asked me if there was anything that I wanted to check in particular. I pondered and then decided to mention the little 'fit' and asked if it meant anything. She referred me to a specialist who asked me a lot of profiling questions before prescribing two types of pills; one to be taken on a regular basis and one only when I was not getting any sleep.

Later, at the customary smoke break, Dev asked me, 'What kind of pills are those?'

'Anti-depressants, I believe. The doc told me clearly that it can't be epilepsy. So, I am in the clear.'

'Anti-depressants! You know what we can do with them?'

Alex made a face. 'Come on, guys. You are treating yourself to enough alcohol. You can't be doing pills and shit.'

Dev responded, 'Why not? It wouldn't be everyday that you will have access to such pills. Our boy has the prescription, so we can try it out. Once can't hurt.'

'Three years of smoking weed and popping pills, and I have done enough of this shit. I will just watch.' Alex bailed out.

'Me too, man. This is just way out of my league.' Arjuna nodded.

Dev turned to the last man that was me. 'What do you think?'

'Once?'

'Once.'

'Okay. Maybe this weekend.'

Dev was ecstatic. 'We have to make it a big one. We need to have girls. Actually a lot of girls. I need to start working on that right away.' With that, he walked back to the office purposefully, followed by the rest of us.

I was concerned about the insidious boredom and so I decided that I might as well work on my project. To my surprise, I had three e-mails promising the spreadsheet model in response to my request on the online forum. I interacted with them over Messenger. One sounded more serious than others and I asked him to demonstrate the model. He was from the Netherlands. I was delighted when I saw the model for it seemed exactly the type required. I paid him using PayPal. I spent the rest of the day in familiarising myself with it so I could answer any tough questions. Now, I had a prototype ready and I decided to show off my efficiency to my boss. I walked to him with a proposal.

'I was thinking about the approach for the spreadsheet model. I thought it will be a good idea to develop a prototype and then ask a few users to use it for some time, so that we will get to know soon enough if there are any bugs in it, or if it is sufficiently user-friendly.' I ventured.

'Why, that is a nice idea. When can you have your prototype ready?'

'I have the basic skeleton ready. I just have to pimp it up a bit and then maybe we can share it with a sample group of users. Do you have any suggestions how many I should invite and how long we should test it?' Inwardly, I asked him to kiss my toes. He didn't disappoint.

'You have a prototype ready? Wow! That's good progress. Why don't you let me talk to a few people by tomorrow and then I will let you know who can be the sample users. I think we may have to test it out in a few countries before we roll it out.'

'Great.'

'The question is, what will you do for those three weeks? We might have to find you an alternate project. Let me think about it.' I kicked myself for not having seen this complication but I quickly recovered and replied, 'I think it would be best if I spend some time with these users so I could really understand the potential improvement areas.'

'Okay. Let's see. Have a good evening then.'

I decided to take a walk back to the apartment as opposed to taking a cab. I took long and purposeful strides even though there wasn't much to do back at the apartment. Somehow, I felt that I should hide my idleness behind a busy exterior and so I tried. I crossed the busy intersection right outside my office and started walking on the footpath on the left. It was lined with trees and carpeted with grass. The trees were swaying in tandem with the strong and moisture-laden wind. It was probably going to rain soon. On my left, there was a row of small shop-houses which later gave way to high-rise condominiums. On my right, the road was busy with the traffic on both the sides moving at high speeds. I put on my headphone tuned to the local radio station which was playing a song from another era.

Runaway Train never going back…wrong way on a one-way track…

Seems like I should be getting somewhere…

Somehow I am neither here nor there…

It was noisy because of the traffic and the wind. I seemed to be alternately swaying to either side depending upon the direction the zipping vehicle that passed me was going. It was also the story of my life. I tried to recall the last time when I had made an important but independent choice. I searched in every closet of my mental faculties but I could not find any such instance.

Can you help me remember how to smile…make it somehow all seem worthwhile…

How on earth did I get so jaded…life's mystery seems so faded…

I thought of taking an alternate approach of working backwards, and counted all the important decisions of my life. There was the time when I had decided to pursue post graduate studies but it was just following in the footsteps of my brother and for lack of anything better to do. There was the decision to join this company but then again, I asked myself if it was really a choice or more a convenient way out. I had done my internship here, which was followed with a job offer. Immediately after that, I had opted out of the campus placement process. It wasn't like I tried to find anything better; rather, I just took the handy option. For my life, I could not find any other important milestones. I thought long and hard and realised that the real important choice, although not independent, had been to move out of Jaipur. My current state of affairs owed a lot to that decision. Although, I reckoned that I wouldn't go back in time and change that decision, but there was no doubt. That had been the only turning point. It seemed so unfair. I was original. I had promise. I was meant for something big, something glamorous. I was supposed to be special but here I was, worse than mediocre. And I silently smiled at myself because how could there be anything worse than mediocre.

I can go where no one else can go…I know what no one else knows…

Here I am just drownin' in the rain…with a ticket for a runaway train…

Was it my fault? Did I miss the turn to greatness? How could the universe entrust me with such a big decision, to begin with?

'Watch where you are going, mister,' shouted a female voice as she hurried past me.

She had bumped into me from behind, for I had halted in my stride. I didn't register what she looked like but the words had a profound effect on me. I didn't know where I was going, leave alone figuring out a way to get there. I was purposeless and therefore, uneasy. What was even worse was that I couldn't quite decide whether to be proud of it or to be ashamed of it. When I compared it with my content father, I found it to be almost original. But to what avail? I could remain fidgety for the rest of my life and it would amount to nothing but a self-justified attempt to dispel mediocrity. Compared to that, at least my father was happy if not authentic.

I found myself walking again. I was happy to realise that I was still on track but then smiled at the irony of it. I took off my headphone and started running. There was no reason for it. I was overly dressed for running, too, but I just wanted to. There was a lady with two kids who gawked at me and grabbed her kids protectively. I felt that she could read my thoughts as she tried to protect her kids, for maybe I was contagious and she would not want her kids to grow up to be like me. I ran faster, till I was breathlessly standing in front of the lift to my apartment. I went straight up, blamed my tortured mental state on lack of sleep, took a sleeping pill and turned into a pile on the couch.

Arjuna woke me up just in time for dinner. I checked my watch. I had been asleep for about two hours. I felt better but still drowsy.

While rubbing my head, I thought aloud, 'I think I might take the day off tomorrow.'

'You slept through the complete first half on Monday. Then, while the rest of us did our medical check-up on the weekend, you used up another half workday for yours. At this rate, you might not make it, mate.'

'I know. You are right. I can't take the day off. I will have to pull myself together.'

'What's your plan for dinner?'

'I am catching up with Bala at a nearby restaurant. She must have arrived by now.'

'I thought she was in India?'

'So did I. Apparently, her job involves a bit of travelling. Anyway, you have a nice one. I will catch you later.'

I stepped out on the road and waited for a cab. There was none forthcoming. So, I walked. My phone rang. To my dismay, it was Radha.

'Hi,' she said in a soft whispery manner. I shuddered at her tone. I was sure that my evening was spoiled.

'Hi back to you. How are you?' I tried desperately to think of how to lead this conversation towards something unimportant.

'Okay. How are things with you?' She sniffed. Uh oh, she seemed to be crying. I kicked myself and almost felt condemned to some uncomfortable talk but not before I made a last-ditch effort. I said, 'Very well. You have a cold or something?'

'No. I am fine.' She sniffed again. Suddenly I grew weary of this little game but kept quiet and let it unfold. It was clear that something was wrong but I didn't want to find out what it was. Probably I did know but I couldn't be bothered. She continued, after a pause, 'You didn't reply to my e-mail.'

'Yeah. I've been kinda busy. Besides, private e-mails are banned in office,' I lied.

She persisted, 'Why don't you give me your office mail id, then?'

I continued lying, 'I think they monitor the office mail id and we have been strictly told that we can't use it for personal things.'

'Okay. Then we will just have to use the phone more often, won't we?'

'Yeah, I guess so.' I was cornered. I would have much preferred the e-mailing as it gave me the opportunity to reply in a measured way and whenever I wanted. This was the second time I was cornered on the same day and I admonished myself to be more circumspect in future. There was silence for a while.

'What happened?' She complained, 'It seems you have nothing to talk about.'

'Things change. I haven't really been having the time of my life around here.'

'I can understand. You must be feeling lonely.'

I didn't like the tone. 'No. I am not.'

'Then?'

'Then what?'

'Then what's wrong?'

'Nothing's wrong.'

'You are talking in riddles. If you want, I could come there for a few days. You know, sort things out.'

'No. That is not required.'

'You don't want to meet me?'

'I won't have time. It's pretty hectic at the moment.' I was getting quite good at lying.

'Is there someone else?'

'No, I am walking by myself for dinner.'

'You know what I mean.'

I wondered whether I should take this opportunity to confess, wrongly of course, that I had found someone else and thereby put an end to this drama. 'No, there isn't.'

'Then what's wrong. Do you still love me?'

'I am not sure.' This was my first honest response during the call.

'What do you mean, you are not sure?' She was almost yelling, 'If you are not sure, then it probably means that you don't love me.'

'Maybe you are right.'

'So what do you want me to do?'

'Find a nice boy and marry him.'

The line went dead.

'That was easy,' I said to myself, breathed a sigh of relief and waited for the first pangs of guilt to hit me. But it didn't. What did hit me was a sense of liberation as if I had switched from tight underpants to boxers. Presently, I walked into the fish-and-chips restaurant with a huge banner outside announcing its seafood platter at a discount. There was a staircase leading to the eating area upstairs while the drinking area was around me. It was filled with noise coming from the traffic on the right. There were clouds of tobacco smoke, mixed with the scent of jasmine flowers which lined the ubiquitous man-made stream on the extreme right. I had already learnt about the auspicious importance of water in every Chinese establishment but the stream continued to affect my mind for some reason. The place was full and with some difficulty, I spotted Bala at an insulated corner table, along with a thickly-moustached person whom I did not recognise.

I placed myself next to Bala and tried to smile apologetically, 'Hey. Sorry I'm late. Couldn't find a cab.'

Bala smiled back, 'This is the second time I've heard that tonight.'

'Come on, babe. You ought to let me off the hook now. At least, I came before he did,' her companion said.

Bala giggled, 'Not many men will boast about that fact.' When none of us responded in the expected manner, she proceeded to explain, 'Came before he did, hello?' The man turned pink.

'Hi, don't believe we have met. Name's Achet. You?'

He shook my hand and held it as he appraised me, 'I am Suraj. I am the Sales Director in the same company as Bala. Achet, a weird name, wouldn't you say?'

'I get that a lot. I used to faint a lot in pre-school and when my teacher sadistically suggested this name, my illiterate parents accepted it without any thought.' He continued to eye me before eventually letting go of my hand.

Bala chimed in, 'Any longer and I would have thought that the absence of your wife has made you swing over to the other side.' At Suraj's questioning look, she added, 'The handshake, mister.'

I felt there was something amiss between the two of them and muttered, 'Layered.'

This time, Suraj turned his questioning look at me. 'Layered?'

I poured myself a glass of beer from the half-empty jug and answered, 'I mean Bala's jokes. They are layered.'

'Yes, Sherlock Holmes. But exactly, what did you mean by layered?'

Not wanting to be left behind in the wit department, I said 'Elementary, Dr. Watson…' but before I could finish my sentence, he boiled over and turned to Bala. 'Who is this guy? Doesn't he know how to talk to people?' Then he turned back to me, 'You might have grown up in a cave with wolves but do realise that now you are in the company of civilised people.'

I was taken aback with this outburst and meekly said, 'Of course.'

'Of course?' He turned incredulous, 'He says of course. Wah! An apology would have been in order, whatsyourname.'

I took the easy way out. 'And I do apologise. I will be careful next time around.'

Bala was slightly amused watching this exchange but she didn't say anything. We sipped our beers in silence punctuated intermittently by the zipping cars against the backdrop of running water.

'I miss my car,' Bala said, in an obvious attempt to break the silence.

Suraj responded, 'How could you miss a car, here in Singapore? You can get cabs everywhere. The public transportation system is also pretty good.'

'Yeah? And still we have two out of three people here who were late because of no cabs.' Bala made quotation marks to emphasise 'no cabs'. 'Unless you guys were original enough to come up with the same excuse.'

'You know when you beat something too many times, it turns flat.'

Bala raised her hands, 'Alright, I'm sorry. We should change the topic. How are things with you, Achet? Liking Singapore so far?'

'Well, it takes some getting used to. So far, so good.'

Suraj interrupted, 'Singapore is the best place for singles. You should make the most of it.'

'And how would you know? As far as I know, you were married before you moved here,' Bala questioned. 'Weren't you?'

Suraj smiled, 'You forget that my wife is still back in India.'

'What's the plan? When is she moving here?'

'What's the hurry?' Suraj shrugged, 'It's not like I miss her or anything.'

Bala was genuinely surprised or maybe it was an act. 'You don't miss your wife?'

'Well, the only thing I miss is sex which is fairly abundant in this part of the world anyway.' Suraj smiled in a proud manner. 'I think it grows on trees around here.'

'You are not saying what I think you are saying, are you?' Bala leaned forward with her elbows on the table. 'You are cheating on your wife?'

'Now, what do you really mean by cheating? If satisfying your body desires is cheating, then I am cheating even as I drink here without her. Really, sex is totally overrated in that aspect. Personally, I don't think I am cheating if I sleep with somebody purely for the physical sex aspect. Emotionally, I am attached only to her.'

'Makes you wonder what else is going around here,' I said.

'You would be surprised, my dear,' Bala answered me and turned her attention back to Suraj. 'I wonder if your wife feels the same way.'

Suraj responded, 'I hope not.'

'Double standards, eh?'

'Not really. Even if she does, I am going to be okay with it. I just wouldn't want to know about it.'

I let out a small but audible laugh. Suraj didn't particularly like it. 'What are you laughing about? When you are as old as I am and as wise, you would realise that there is nobody who hasn't cheated, in the conventional sense of the word, at least once on their partners. It is part of life out here. This is the new morality.'

'Maybe you are right. I am only a week old around here. And I do understand you just didn't mean Singapore. You probably meant the high-handed corporate uppity league, where the educated elite belong. But I am a novice even in that department. And please don't crucify me for I am not pre-supposing that I belong in that league. In fact, I would rather I didn't. But I probably do. Time will tell.'

Bala beckoned, 'Are you afraid of him, Achet? Speak freely. Tell him to, Suraj.' Suraj gave me a nod.

'See, it is none of my business what you consider morally right or wrong. I mean, it is just a personal demarcation anyway, isn't it? I would have frowned upon it myself about two weeks ago but I almost made a pass at a girl last night, and it wasn't like I was single.'

'You made a pass? What exactly happened,' Bala asked.

'That doesn't matter. The intent was there. So, in a way, I have already cheated on my girlfriend. And I didn't feel any guilt about that either. So, I can understand when Suraj says what he says. However, at the same time, I don't think it's right. For two reasons: one, you yourself said, Suraj, that you wouldn't want to know if your wife was sleeping around. If you were truly open-minded, for lack of a better word, you would not mind it. In fact, you might even actually plan it with your wife and take the pleasure to another level. But the fact that you wouldn't want to know about it means that you would be hurt, however slightly, if you did get wind of it. That is probably a good enough factor to conclude that seeking sex elsewhere is not considered right by your subconscious. You think or more like, hope it is natural but you know that it isn't.' I paused to take a sip of beer.

Then I continued. 'I think the first reason in itself is a good enough measure of what constitutes morality or immorality and that too, on your own personal scale. But I will offer you a second reason as well. If you are seeking physical pleasure or companionship elsewhere without the slightest guilt, then that's fine. It probably means that there is something wrong in your relationship with your wife. Maybe you are an eternal bachelor or a playboy, or gay. Nothing wrong with any of this, as long as the remorse is absent. But if you have to somehow come up with a virtuous rationalisation to justify these activities to yourself and to those around you, then in my opinion, you have crossed your own moral confines. You are better off confronting it, rather than playing along.'

If Suraj was furious, he did a good job of hiding it. He was definitely agitated, for he couldn't figure out what to say. Bala seemed to repent having asked me for my opinion. She put her hand on top of his on the table to signal calm. But he withdrew and massaged his forehead a few times as if suffering from a headache, while looking down at his beer glass. He eventually found speech. 'You are a presumptuous little bastard. You don't know what it is out there. When you are working your ass off in a job with the punchline 'same shit different day'. When you are forced to have your dinner by yourself in a hurry because you don't want anybody to see you eating alone. In fact, you go out of your way to find inconspicuous places where you know that you won't be noticed, but you still worry nonetheless. And at night, when you have nothing but pillows besides you, you will know what I am talking about.'

He grabbed his glass, drained it, refilled it and took a larger gulp still.

Bala's attempts at pacifying him changed from mere gestures to words. 'You have probably been drinking too much. Take it easy. Achet didn't really mean anything serious. Tell him, Achet.' I half-nodded and she added, 'In fact, how the hell does it matter, anyway.'

Suraj ignored Bala's advice and finished another glass. As the jug was empty now, he spotted a waitress and asked for another pitcher.

Seeing that her efforts with Suraj were fruitless, Bala turned to me. 'So you think you can fight temptation?'

'I never said that.'

Bala threw up her hands, 'Then what was your speech about?'

'I was just pointing out the anomaly between Suraj's doings and his moral principles, insofar as I could make out.'

'Bull.' She summarily dismissed my argument. 'And you, yourself? Didn't you say you made a pass at a girl?'

'Yes. I admit to that.'

'And that does not qualify as going against your lofty principles?'

'Those are not my principles, Bala. Those are Suraj's principles, as far as I could deduce. You can't judge a person against somebody else's moral scale. Morality is relative. You can judge me against my principles, if I have any, that is.' I sniggered at the last statement, 'but as I told you, I didn't feel any remorse. So it is likely that my standards are more relaxed. Besides, I have since broken up with her.'

'What? You broke up with her just because you made a pass at somebody else?'

'Not, because of only that. That was just a wake-up call. As I mentioned before, something was wrong in my relationship. I couldn't see any other way out.'

'You are a strange man.'

I reflected, 'It is better to be stranger to others than to oneself.'

Bala eyed me for some time before saying, 'Something tells me that you are a stranger to yourself, too.'

That was the most intelligent statement Bala had made that night. How many times does it happen that something very profound comes out from a source least expected? You are watching a run-of-the-mill movie, but there is one view hidden that is suddenly revealed and that makes it all worthwhile. You are reading an utter banal book and the one-dimensional plot throws up a major possibility that sweeps you off your feet. You are being forced to bear a lengthy conversation with a person you classify an utter bore, and suddenly he enlightens you with a meaningful philosophical utterance.

What is perhaps more important is that you are not sure if anyone else has made the same discovery as you have just done. In fact, even the person making that observation may not be aware of its significance. Sometimes, as in this particular case, it is so because the observation is contextually significant from your viewpoint. On numerous other occasions, however, the subject utters the observation so as to justify his existence or so as to be considered equal to his audience whom he has subconsciously designated as higher beings. But since he does so with an ulterior motive, the significance of his own observation fails to dawn upon him.

'I'm going to make a move.' Suraj made way to get up and motioned Bala, 'You wanna come with me?'

'Don't you wanna have dinner?'

'No. I'm going to call it a night. Take care.' He left hurriedly without as much as a nod towards me.

Bala proceeded to pour herself a glass of beer, 'Congratulations. That will take you a long way in this company.'

'I thought he asked for my opinion. By the way, by when does one reach the level of a Director?' I tried to assess the damage.

'Well, let's say if you do really well, you can get there in about a decade. That is the record that Suraj himself set.' Bala turned mischievous, 'However, at the rate you are going currently, you may set the record for the fastest time in which a person can get fired.'

'Not very politically correct, was I? You couldn't have tried to steer the conversation somewhere else?'

Bala considered her naked fingernails, 'I could have. But I didn't really want to. Suraj is an asshole and he deserved that.'

'So, I was right.'

'You mean you identified the asshole in him from the start? Then this must be your secret superhero identity when you save the world from assholes at night. Is that correct?'

Smiling, I said, 'No. That's not what I meant. It is just that I found something layered between you two.'

'And what do you think was the layer?'

'How would I know? You tell me.'

Bala turned her attention to her fingernails again, 'There is nothing there, really. He propositioned me some time ago and asked me if I could be his companion whenever I am here, and while his wife is elsewhere.' I raised my eyebrows, 'And yes, that meant a sex partner. But don't let your imagination run wild. I refused.'

I drank from my glass, 'I'm sure you did.'

'Why? You don't believe me?'

We were interrupted by the waitress who reminded us that the kitchen was about to close, and if we wanted to eat, this would be a good time to place an order.

'I am not hungry. Achet, you wanna order something?'

'Neither am I, but thanks for checking.' The waitress smiled and left.

I continued, 'No, I do believe you. This probably explains why he bared himself so much in front of a total stranger like me. He must have tried explaining those emotions with you before and was trying his luck yet again. And he couldn't care less about what I thought of it. To top it all, you didn't leave with him. And I can see your excuse of having dinner was a false one. Tomorrow morning, he is going to feel sore about it. Crap! That means the damage is going to be even deeper. You should have left with him and offered him a blow-job for his efforts. That could have saved my job.'

Bala simpered, 'You are funny.'

'So what is this I hear about you being a morally-challenged person and all?'

'What?' She was genuinely shocked.

'Sorry, I must have heard wrong or lent my ear to the wrong people, I guess.' I realised that I had taken one step too far here. It was clearly not a day where my social etiquette fared well.

Bala continued to look at me in disbelief and mumbled, 'No. You have heard right. I was just shocked by the directness of the question. Not so much about the accusation.'

'Hey, I'm not accusing you of anything. I am just trying to clarify whether it was true or not. Frankly, I don't give a damn about it. I like you as a person and as far as I am concerned, this part of your life doesn't matter.'

'It is true. Rather, it was true. In my younger reckless days, I have done things that I am not very proud of. I have been trying to change my ways.'

'Change, in what sense?' I lit a cigarette.

'I want to marry and settle down. My mother is trying to set me up with eligible bachelors or at least, those she claims are eligible bachelors. Let's see.'

'You mean, like an arranged marriage?'

'Yes. Why, any problems with that?' She glared at me.

'Why do you always take on this accusing tone? I'm on your side, hello?'

'I'm sorry. It's just that after years of being misunderstood and pointed out, I'm now guarded most of the time. Besides, you know what they say about arranged marriage? That it's for losers.'

'I understand. To set the record straight, I don't think arranged marriage is for losers at all. After all, they have a very successful track record.'

We continued drinking and chatting for another couple of hours. I thought that there was a bit of flirting involved but I couldn't be sure. I considered making a more direct move and I almost did, when I dropped her back in a shared cab but words failed me.

In one day, I had made a mockery of professional ethics, walked out on a long-term girl friend, and had almost committed career suicide. The surprising part was that I didn't care about any of it. Self-destruction had never sounded so glamorous to me. It was only the following weekend that I realised that the rest of the guys were even further up ahead on the same road.

◆

9

Mediocre but Aware

The weekend had arrived and the weekend warriors were at work, overtime, to corner as many pretty girls as possible. None of them had started on their mission as early as Dev. However, for all his efforts, he could manage only one girl but that was enough to impart a reasonable amount of diversity to a party which otherwise could have been another disturbing male bonding session. Not that I minded male bonding; in fact, I preferred conversations in smaller groups, irrespective of their sexual origins or inclinations. In this particular instance, however, it didn't matter because I had taken half-a-dozen pills and was reasonably numb to any dialogue. So had Dev, but the effect on him seemed to be, thankfully, cheerful. We had voted, Dev's words had prevailed, and we were in the balcony, playing drinking games.

However, before that, let me introduce the participants in the crime. The party was hosted by Dev at our apartment. The usual suspects, namely, Alex, Arjuna and myself, were of course, present. The beauty quotient was augmented by Bala. We were seated around the glass table with the plastic translucent top.

Thankfully, the apartment across the street was deserted. The boys had formed some ground-rules beforehand. We had agreed that since there was only one girl available between four of us, sacrifice was called for. I didn't really stand a chance against the bulging biceps of Arjuna or the conventionally fair and well-proportioned facial contours of Dev and Alex. Thus, I had stepped aside and left it to them to figure out how they wanted to play it. Further, I had wanted to keep it as an element of surprise for myself and had barred the boys from letting me know of their plans. I wanted to be as unsuspecting as Bala herself.

Soon, it was past midnight and we were playing 'I have never', a game wherein participants took turns in uttering a statement which began with 'I have never' and whoever had done whatever the speaker hadn't, had to drink. For example, I might say, `I have never had sex' and whoever is not a virgin would have to drink up. Needless to say, the game was initially meant to get to know others better but it had turned out to be a ploy to listen in on the sexual experiences of others. I had so far drunk to most of the statements without really listening to them, only because I wanted to drink.

Bala was eating a slice of pizza. She was feeling bored and made no bones about letting it show. 'These are all quite silly games, really. Do I look like I give a damn whether Alex has had a threesome or whether Dev can last for an hour?'

'What would you rather do then?' Arjuna enquired.

'I don't know. This is not my party, is it, mister?'

Arjuna barked back, 'Don't you mister me, missy.'

'Why don't we just go around the table and ask questions that you are interested in? That way, Arjuna can ask if anybody has had anal sex while Bala can ask the meaning of life, universe and everything,' Alex tried to placate them.

'That sounds fair to me,' Arjuna said as he quaffed some wine. 'Why don't we start with Bala?'

'Why me?'

'Because you wanted to change the flow. Didn't you?'

'I would rather wait for my turn.'

Alex continued to mediate. 'Alright. We need somebody neutral. Dev, you wanna start?'

'There is nobody more neutral than you here, Alex. But I don't mind starting,' Dev said. I was pleased by Bala's intervention. Honestly, the whole evening had been so sprinkled with sex, to the verge of being obsessive. Dev posed his question. 'Are you guys happy with the way you have turned out?' Dev had decided to turn philosophical, not surprisingly. I recalled this question as one of the only two questions from the Happiness survey that I had read somewhere the previous week.

There were protests from all. `Don't spoil the party, mate. I drank a full bottle of wine and I have already sobered down,` said Arjuna. Even Bala made a face. Alex interjected once again. 'You asked for it and agreed to it. You have got to answer it. Let me add two more rules, though. One, no judgment, please, and two, you can decline to answer a maximum of one question but you have to drink up, in lieu. Quick, keep it short and simple.'

Alex then volunteered to reply first. 'I don't believe in reflecting on the past. I believe that whatever choices you made at various points of time are the best possible choices that you could have made within the limitations of the circumstances and your own personal prejudices and shortcomings. As such, I would never repent anything I have done or not done. I have made mistakes but I have learned from them. And so I guess, I would say that I am fairly satisfied with my life so far.'

Dev was next. 'I am not happy but I am satisfied with my life. You can call me an underachiever. It is a label that I have always been attached to. I believe that I am far more talented than a lot of my peers but ironically they have accomplished much more than I have. Sometimes I feel that the whole universe is against me. The only thing that I am proud of is my 'bouncebackability.' There hasn't been a setback that I haven't been able to bounce back from. So much so that I feel glorious when I look back at how I have negotiated some rough terrain so far. The bad thing about it is that I have never had any time to admire the landscape and have always had to focus on the milestones. However, now it seems that my time has come and this job is a testimony to that. I am the only one who has been selected from my university. Hell, they don't even recruit from my university, it being considered too inferior. But I have transcended all odds and now, here I am.'

It was Bala's turn now. I looked forward to a blunt and honest answer and she didn't disappoint. 'Frankly, I am not satisfied with my life. I have made some wrong choices that were not totally driven by circumstances or anything. Those were purely wrong judgments on my part. I wish I could look back and say that I learned from those mistakes but the truth is that I have made the same mistakes over and over again. I wish I had devoted more time to my autistic sister. I wish I were married by now and not branded a slut. No, no, don't look so horrified. I know you are all aware that I'm called such; some of you may have even contributed to it.' She ignored the protests and continued. 'Whether you did or said that is immaterial. Because I don't blame you. I have had it coming.' She paused for some wine, inspected her fingernails which were painted a pale purple. 'Then again, there are some positives to take away from my life; for example, I regard myself quite successful in my career. But, unfortunately, I have been successful in departments that I would have to classify as unimportant, while in all the important areas, I have come out a dud. However, I still wouldn't want to re-live my life. I am afraid I might make an even bigger mess of it. Even if I were able to salvage a few things, I still wouldn't do it, for the only thing going for me at this time is my misery. At least I have something to cling on to, a constant companion to live my life by. Really, misery can be a welcome parasite even if it does suck the life out of you. It's just that, in my case, I derive my desire to go on from it. How ironic, my misery sucking my life out of me and me deriving my will to live from it. Actually, I correct myself, for it's not a parasite in my case. I believe the term is symbiosis. In fact, I am so dependent upon it that I believe some of my wrong choices have been inadvertent attempts to fan more misery. I hate to admit it but I thrive on misery.' She stopped short, looking straight at me but I knew that her sight was impervious to objects, living or dead and she was looking through me, beyond me. 'That's all I have to say.'

There was silence. I thought I heard a moth buzzing around the street light. For a moment, I wondered if somehow the pills had found their way into Bala's drink. Dev made a feeble attempt at adding sonic waves to the dark matter around, 'Come on, it can't all be that bad. I am sure there are a lot of good things around you and because of you.'

'No judgment, Dev. Arjuna, your turn.' Alex intervened.

'That's a difficult one.' Arjuna paused to puff at his dying cigarette. He dropped the ashes in his wine and drank deeply, 'I think I am happy to have turned out the way I am as a person. However, I am not happy with what I have accomplished so far. Does that make any sense?'

There was a murmur of assent and he continued, 'I am not very ambitious. To me, my career is just a means of achieving what really matters. I think with this job, my career is on the right track. However, I haven't really done anything about what really matters to me. In fact, I am on the verge of stepping beyond the irretrievable. If I need to make any changes, the time is fucking now.'

I asked on behalf of the group, 'What is it that you want to do?'

'You are aware of it, so don't be a smartass. But for the sake of the rest of the group: I want to contribute to the well-being of the Tamils in Lanka. I wish I could do something about that. Anyways, the circle is complete. It's your turn now, mate.'

I answered sheepishly, 'To be honest, I don't know if I am happy to have turned out the way I have but I don't think I would have it any other way.'

Multiple sets of eyes kept looking at me expectantly and when nothing else came forth, Bala finally complained, 'This is so not fair. We bared our souls here and you try to be cool. That makes you a bloody pretender, mister. At least use your veto, if you don't want to answer the question.'

Alex was smiling and tried to see the lighter side of it, 'I think we should give you a middle name 'I-don't-know.' I wouldn't be surprised if tomorrow you murder somebody without knowing why.'

I responded, 'Really, this is how I feel. If you want, you can probe more. Ask away. Maybe that way, even I will get clarity.'

Bala was still feeling a little cheated and articulated her irritation quite cogently. 'We are not going to treat you like a fucking celebrity sitting on an Oprah talk show. You can go into a corner and fuck yourself, for all I care.'

'That wouldn't be necessary. Let me say more.' I reckoned that I was obligated to explain myself. 'Arjuna and I have talked about it before. Really, life is more of a quest for me, to find some purpose. I am not there yet. I know that I am on a quest but I also know that I am more likely to die of old age than of finding some meaning. So, clearly, I am not happy. But I am not sad, either. I am happy because I realise the quest is on but I am sad because the meaning of the quest eludes me. So, I would say that I am probably dissatisfied.'

Arjuna asked as he leaned back in his chair while holding his cigarette tantalisingly close to his lips, 'Why do you say then that you wouldn't have it any other way?'

'Because I consider myself one of the lucky few to be blessed with this awareness of being unaware. I don't think I am unique in being unaware but I consider myself unique in being aware of the fact. Most live their lives feeling something is amiss. I look around me and nobody seems to have done anything about it.' I lit a cigarette and continued. 'Most are in a state of denial. Some go to the next level, and argue and convince themselves that it is futile to slot that vague feeling into any mind-space. Very few actually confront it and reconcile with it. If you think you belong to the last group, then that realisation itself ought to be celebrated and is good enough justification not to live your life over again.

Because if you do that, the law of averages suggests that you will turn out to be another head in the mob, somebody you would have ridiculed in today's life.'

Alex re-phrased Arjuna's question. 'But surely, with the benefit of hindsight and allowing for time travel, you could potentially go back and change what you don't like?'

'That is the whole irony. I don't know what went wrong where. Hell, I don't even know if something did, indeed, go wrong. I have a strong suspicion that my salvation lies not in the past but in the future. What I need to change is not how I have turned out to be but rather what I am going to do about it now. And so I wouldn't wanna go back and change my life. I am satisfied with the way I am but I am still dissatisfied because I don't know where to go from here. If that makes any sense. I am where I don't want to be. I can't be where I want to be because I don't know where that is.'

For some time, we sipped our wine and smoked our cigarettes without saying anything. A lot had already been said. It seemed that despite the fact that we were crammed into a small space, at that moment, we were all alone, pondering over our intangible lives. This was a luxury that I hadn't experienced in the past with any group. Previously, there had always been intruders, spoiling an otherwise mysteriously profound moment being shared by a few people. You could find the intruders everywhere, in every group and in every setting. They would hide behind a carefully woven glamorous veil, shielding themselves from scrutiny but would be always and almost too quick and eager to judge others for the slightest show of vulnerability. I considered myself extremely fortunate that I was in a mature group where one wasn't afraid to be oneself, where everyone was original but originality still wasn't a prerequisite for admission.

'I am waiting to see who shows the first signs of being suicidal and jumps off the ledge,' Arjuna quipped and laughed aloud at his own joke. Others did too, but more as a reaction to his laughter than to the wit-quotient of the remark. It broke the moment but I didn't mind it. He continued, 'I am going to ask a question now. Who are we likely to sleep with in the office?'

Bala responded, 'That's very easy. You will obviously be sleeping with Achet. That so?'

'No, no. It has to be somebody from the opposite sex. You first.' This was clearly one of the fall-back strategies that the boys must have worked among themselves in case the night fell flat. I leaned back, ready to be amused as Bala exercised her veto. When the boys' turn came, Dev named Bala while the rest of us picked the Filipina chick.

We continued with similar games till late. I faded out soon and retired to the bedroom. Next morning, in the boys-only debrief session, I learnt that Bala cock-teased Dev for as long as he continued his pursuit before eventually abandoning the game and him. All of us agreed that he deserved it, knowing that it was he who had introduced the dreadful topic and made sure that nobody had any fun thereafter.

Looking back, our friendship was forged that night when we bared ourselves to each other. But I was soon to find out how little we really understood each other.

10

Transmogrification

It was late Sunday morning and I was having breakfast at a place called Toast. There was a bit of an argument in the morning when we were debating where to have our next meal. Arjuna and Alex wanted to try out a new burger place while Dev wanted to check out this particular place. We had decided to split up, agreeing to rejoin later at Starbucks for a coffee. Bala had joined us at Toast as well. I had ordered a chicken wrap and a glass of orange juice while Bala and Dev had ordered a chicken caesar salad and a cup of tea each. I wasn't in the mood for any conversation, so I hid behind a newspaper.

Bala asked me, 'You aren't very social, are you?'

Dev replied on my behalf. 'He is like that in the mornings. He is a nocturnal creature. We all are, aren't we?'

'Still, if you are sitting with other people, you can't just switch off,' Bala complained, and I gave in. 'Sure. What do you want to talk about?'

'That's exactly what I meant. You are too confrontational and blunt. This is not how normal people talk to each other,' Bala said, sipped her tea and added after a pause, 'But to be honest, I kind of like how guileless and straightforward you are. Your parents have brought you up well.'

Dev finished the last of his salad as he said, 'Really, do you think it is all a matter of upbringing? I read somewhere that genetics and surroundings play a far larger role in a person's development than his upbringing. If I remember right, they had actually conducted an experiment by looking at adopted children and had concluded that they grew up to be similar to their biological parents and not their adopted parents.'

I was intrigued and followed up with a question. 'What do you mean by surroundings?'

'I don't remember the exact details as I had read that article a long time back. But they concluded that a child's friends, his school, college and other external environmental factors play a far greater role than the parents themselves.' He wiped his mouth with tissue paper and discarded it on the table. 'If I am not mistaken, they had studied two groups of black kids from similar socio-economical backgrounds, one group raised in a decent neighbourhood while the other raised in crime-ridden black ghettos and streets.'

'Interesting,' I said, 'I have always thought that our education system churns out clones running in the same rat-race, with no diversity of interests or thoughts. Your theory validated it. After all, if the system is homogenous, more or less, it is bound to churn out clones.'

Bala responded, 'Come on. Everybody blames the Indian education system. That has become the fashionable thing to do nowadays.'

Dev came out in my support. 'Achet is right. I mean, just look at it. Our education system is very much geared towards academic excellence with no weightage for extra-curricular activities. I mean I was an all-rounder in college but I still couldn't make it through to the business schools because they thought I wasn't worthy.'

'Let's keep our personal prejudices out of it and have a constructive debate, shall we?' Bala intervened. 'The Indian education system has its faults but at least it is based upon meritocracy. Anybody who is good enough can make it regardless of where he comes from or how poor he is. Just look at Achet. He comes from a small town, never been out of Jaipur and from what I understand, his family isn't very well off either. But he is still here with us.'

'Good enough? Huh? And who decides who is good and who is not? Achet, who continuously topped his classes, is good and I, who never topped my classes but had above-average grades nonetheless and who, by the way, was the cricket team captain and was the head of debating society, am not good enough. I say balls to such a system.'

I decided to contribute to the debate. 'Dev is right. If I were the interviewer and I had to choose between him and me, I would have favoured Dev. But the pros and cons that you guys are pointing out probably exist in all kinds of education systems. I mean in the US, you don't just have to be good but also shell out a lot of money to get an education like we get in our business schools. And so, I don't condemn our education system for that. Any system would have such minor glitches. My problem is, however, more basic. I don't think our system allows for diversity or freedom of choice. I mean, I went through the motions of higher education simply because everybody thought it to be the best. If I am in the provinces, I am expected to get out of there and head for the city via higher education. But why exactly do I need to escape provincial life? Is it really that bad? After all, my parents have lived there, as have their parents and they seem to be happy with their state of affairs. But nobody bothered to ask me whether I want to really move to the city. Heck, nobody even bothered to tell me that I needed to pose that question to myself. In fact, the system is such that such questions are considered taboo; so much so that I would kill them the moment they would originate in my subconscious for I would be too embarrassed, otherwise. Now, at that young an age, you need somebody to tell you the importance of such a choice so you can make it knowledgeably. I am afraid that is just not happening currently.'

Bala gave me a confused look and said, 'Come on. You decided on pursuing higher education. Now you have to live with it. You can't blame it on anybody or the system, for that matter.'

'Really, Bala?' I said, 'I agree that it was my decision but was I equipped to make such a decision? Did anybody tell me that by taking such a decision, I would have to live my life in a phoney high society that I would learn to shun, that I would have to work for a multinational corporate entity which is such a façade that I don't even know who is really operating, that I would be forced to withstand and avoid moral temptations on a daily basis. That in the whole process, I might cease to be me. Come on, look at Suraj. He is the most successful guy out there. Didn't you say that? Would I like him as my role model? I don't know, man. I just want the things I know to be the things I knew.'

Bala quipped sarcastically, 'And last night you said that you wouldn't want to change anything about your past.'

I replied, 'I still wouldn't want to do that. The fact that we are having such a conversation itself owes its possibility to the same education system. Besides, now I am here, I might as well experience the other side. Better to get both perspectives before eventually deciding what to do.'

'You are not saying that you could possibly go back to your provinces, are you?'

'No. I am not saying that. Besides, the fact remains that I have probably degenerated too much to be able to fit back there anymore. Then again, I am not ruling that out either.'

Dev reflected, 'We are both so similar and yet so opposite. We suffer from the same system. We both have what the other wants. Anyhow, this Alex bugger has started texting me now. Let's move to Starbucks.'

We paid the bill and moved out. We hailed a cab and arrived at the Starbucks outlet close to our apartment. Alex and Arjuna were sitting outside in the open air alternately sipping their coffee and blowing smoke bubbles. I bought a cappuccino as did the other two, and joined them.

'How was your lunch?' Arjuna asked and Dev replied, 'Actually, quite good. The place has a homely feel. You should try it. How was yours?'

'Ours was pathetic. We should have come with you,' Alex said, 'I reckon Arjuna would have almost killed the chef if I hadn't convinced him otherwise.'

'So how are your projects coming along?' asked Bala. Varying responses followed, Dev's being the most depressing answer while Alex's was the most upbeat.

Alex asked, 'You have gone through the drill before, Bala, haven't you? They say they will confirm our jobs only after six months. But is it really difficult to be confirmed?'

'No, it isn't. You have to be really bad to be disqualified. Most people make it. In my batch, there was only one person who didn't make it. And it was very clear from the beginning that she wouldn't. She wasn't cut out for this kind of a job. The important thing is that you should be able to figure out whether you are cut out for this corporate life or not.'

'I think I am completely cut out for this life. Good money. Cosmopolitan life. High league. This is exactly what I have always dreamed of,' Alex ventured. Dev seconded those sentiments.

Bala proffered, 'It's a little different once you are confirmed. Your honeymoon period is over and as opposed to working on small and short projects, you would be given specific job profiles and the work essentially becomes routine, with a few projects here and there adding to the variety. I guess it is more like running a sprint versus running a marathon. You will have to adjust to that.'

Alex was uncharacteristically vocal today. 'I think I could get used to it. I don't know about others. I guess Dev is also like me. Aren't you, Dev?' Dev nodded. 'You, Arjuna?'

Arjuna said flatly, 'I don't think I can get used to a marathon, man. I need variety. I guess I will see how it goes and then accordingly, I will decide later. I don't have to sign any bond or anything like that, do I, Bala?' Bala shook her head and said, 'No. You are free to leave whenever you want. You just have to give a month's notice. The decision to quit, however, becomes increasingly difficult as you spend more time.'

'How is that?' I asked.

'With every year, your market value relative to your current pay, goes down. It's similar to a brand new car which depreciates fast as soon as it is out of the showroom. Secondly, you become more and more comfortable with the status quo, and become risk-averse. It's like a wild cat which gets used to the zoo and will probably die if left in the wild again.'

'Man, you are getting good at providing metaphors,' I said, grinning.

'Learning from you,' she smiled. 'Anyway, like I was saying before, the most important thing is whether you can get used to it or not. I mean, it's a different ball-game. Doing the same things over and over again. Like Achet was saying earlier, you are working for a faceless and shapeless entity and not for a noble cause or anything but simply for profit.'

'Ah. The age-old capitalism versus socialism conundrum,' Alex said, yawning. 'Ready for an afternoon nap, what say?'

We were being stripped off of our innocence. Slowly, our brains were becoming numbingly accustomed to what we had ridiculed before. The transmogrification was on its way to completion and the best part was that we weren't even aware of it.

11

The Grind

I WAS UNCOMFORTABLY settling into some kind of a routine. It wasn't good. I had bought more time from my boss so that I could 'perfect my little spreadsheet model' and so I had the licence to while away a few days more. I would wake up whenever I could muster enough energy to get out of bed. I would toss a coin to decide whether to shave. Heads meant shaving was on. I loved that bit of uncertainty. But, when heads arrived for three days in a row, I had to abandon that method. From then on, I relied on my mood swings for this important decision. I would almost always walk to the office listening to music. It would be an eleven-minute walk. Most of the time, I was able to listen to two songs in between atrocious jokes cracked by the radio jockey. The days when I could listen to three songs were few and I hated them because I somehow felt that I had used up my luck for the day. I would pause before entering the unavoidable shopping mall en route to the office elevators and let my mood decide whether I would be dodging the inevitable salesmen or whether I would start the day with a frivolous conversation with one of them. Almost always, I would make the latter choice. Sometimes, when I was indecisive, my choice would be made by some unfortunate but aggressive salesman or salesgirl taking the initiative. I would listen to them making an entire sales pitch and would create excuses on the spot for not buying, some downright vulgar. Sometimes, I would just nod, let them talk endlessly and admire their capacity to talk while silently updating my record book for the longest unsuccessful sales-pitch ever. Some of them were really good and could go on for ever. As professional courtesy, I took my excuses really seriously and never repeated them. If I was bored, I would swear in Hindi, dropping a strong hint that I didn't know the language. If it was a pretty sales girl, I would tell her that I would buy the pen-set if she came with it. Once, I offered the person a job as my personal assistant as long as he would lend his arse to me whenever I felt like it.

Eventually, I would disengage myself and move to the office elevators. As I would exit at my floor, I would ensure that I pressed all the floor buttons before disembarking. Sometimes, when I felt lonely, I would press the emergency alarm button and talk to the security. Once on my floor, I would lazily look at the seating map to figure out where I would sit that day. I would look at the little tags with names attached to the virtual cubicles on the wall. Hot-desking was fashionable and so the early bird always got the best seat. My choices would frequently be limited to the cubicle next to the toilets. But before exercising that choice, I would imagine the name-tags to be little cars and my hand would drive them across the map as I provided background sound in little inaudible 'vrooms.' When I thought I had caused sufficient confusion for anybody coming after me, I would move to an empty cubicle.

Sometimes, I would see the name-tag of a particular person that I didn't like and throw it in the dustbin while replacing it with mine. I would then walk to the cubicle occupied by him, claiming that it was mine.

Once at my cubicle, I would turn my computer on and let it boot, as I made myself a cup of tea; half a cup of hot water, an entire sachet of milk powder, two teaspoons of sugar and a tea bag. It would always taste dreadful but I developed a taste for it. Sometimes when the smell wasn't horrible enough, I would make my tea again. I would then come back to my machine and go through my e-mail. My e-mail box would be flooded since others would have had a headstart of at least a couple of hours. As a rule of thumb, I wouldn't spend more than half-an-hour on e-mailing and so when the time was up, I would randomly delete a few of the mails. I reckoned that if anything was important, I would get to know about it, anyway. Later, when anybody asked me about any particular note that I couldn't recall, I would claim that my laptop was unprofessional and sometimes acted of its own accord.

Thus would arrive the most important time of the day, my first smoke break at around 11 a.m. Mostly, I would try to have the break alone. The smoking zone was a small congested area on the ground floor and it would be quite an effort to smoke alone. Often, I would not even return a nod from fellow colleagues and smokers, just to see whether they could exercise adequate self-control to avoid disturbing me. If they didn't, I would limit my contribution to the conversation to 'yeahs' delivered in the form of vicious grunts, designed to repel. On rare occasions when I did enjoy a solitary smoke, I would be inspired into self-analysis that acted as a precursor to the onset of a depressing mood. My mind would gravitate towards abstract thinking but I would force it to map my behaviour into some form of a structure. One such day, I thought about how it was that I could so passionately trivialise everything when in company or when in office and yet feel absolutely miserable when by myself or at night. Then I had to laugh at myself for having used 'passionate' and 'trivialise' in the same sentence. But I continued to be bogged by the seemingly opposite sets of behaviour. I concluded that my frivolity was an escape from myself and was important in a manner that did not reveal itself. Nonetheless, it was crucial for me to keep my feet on the ground while sometimes allowing me dizzying flights of abstraction into the stratosphere.

A few rounds in the office, playing a prank here, a trick there, would ensure that I reached lunch-time without any accomplishment. I found it quite fascinating to note the eating habits of the folks around me. There were some who would bring lunchboxes from home and eat in silence in obscure corners, lest somebody like me decided to invite himself over. Some would eat the same dish over and over again at an appalling South Indian restaurant down the road. Still others would cynically look upon eating as an evil necessity and order takeaway at the ubiquitous McDonalds or Burger King in the shopping mall. A few dared to venture beyond, by eating at the food court or at restaurants specialising in alien cuisine, but only to announce to the world what connoisseurs of good food they were. Lunch, for me, was a leisurely affair, lasting a good one-and-a-half hours. Not because I enjoyed eating but because it meant I could ignore my mental turbulence on the pretext of physical activity. Initially, I would look for company but I soon realised that I bored people to death during such luncheons, and possibly even spread gloom. Besides, others wanted a quicker lunch, so as to get back to their pathetic excuse of work. And so, I graciously started having lunches by myself.

Whenever my boss asked me out for lunch, I would invent vague excuses. When I ran out of such excuses, I told him that I couldn't have lunch with a non-believer, him being a Chinese. To his credit, he took it well. He was probably trying to show off his cultural sensitivity. I would often be seen by colleagues eating alone in a restaurant. Whenever any concerned face approached me and asked me the reason I was eating alone, I would sneeze and blame the flu which ensured the rapid scurrying away of the intruders. Sometimes, I would point to the cover page of the magazine I was reading and say that I was having dinner with Angelina Jolie. Once I confessed that I was a sociopath on Wednesday noons.

I generally considered my productive hours to be done by lunch. I was fairly convinced that this sentiment was shared by the majority of my colleagues, since many of them would indulge in activities unrelated to work. There was a particular Filipina lady who took it upon herself to set up blind dates for lonely and ugly guys and girls. She somehow arrived at the conclusion that I was one such guy and asked me if I would be interested. I told her that I would have been but my parents had married me off at the age of four to a girl who was three months old at the time. She was shocked and proceeded to spend the entire afternoon in trying to convince me that I couldn't possibly stay true to this marriage and that child-marriage was a sin. I vehemently agreed but when I told her that my in-laws would cut off my balls if I bailed out, she gave up. My afternoons, otherwise, would be filled with smoke and coffee breaks. Initially I did it with the whole of my gang but soon I realised that they didn't share the same intensity involved in whiling away time as me. Therefore, I started going for these breaks with one at a time, so as to maximise the number of breaks.

I would dread the evenings and the walk home which somehow, always seemed longer than the eleven minutes it took in the mornings. I wouldn't bother to put music on. I would walk head down, relying entirely on my feet to keep me on track and out of harm's way. Like the clockwork precision of tropical rains, depression would take over. I would daydream about an alien spaceship which had taken over the world and demanded to talk to me because I was mysteriously special. They wouldn't divulge what was special about me. I would be so afraid of finding it out myself that I would stop dreaming about it at that point, and think of something else, like a flirtatious miniskirt or a woman clad only in her heels. I wouldn't be able to concentrate and it would start a lightning chain of thoughts. By the end of the walk, my mind would have moved from alien invasion to sex on a tennis court, or other similarly unlikely events. One evening, I forced myself to trace the link backwards from one thought to another, and developed a headache. Almost every evening, I would toss down a few capsules to stun my brain. I learnt that a paralysed brain didn't mean the absence of thoughts but it did increase my resistance level to bear those thoughts.

Others had been evolving into better examples of corporate citizens. Dev and Alex very rarely came back to the apartment before ten at night. Arjuna was only slightly better. They would always act surprised to see me leave early as though they were expecting much more from me. I couldn't blame them, for I myself was expecting much more from me. Once we got together, we would have our dinner over irrelevant chatter. It would be followed by drinking till the late hours. Sometimes we went to a club. Many-a-time, I got sloshed and misbehaved but I was largely taken care of by somebody or the other. Sometimes, when we felt like staying indoors, we would hang out at the balcony and alternately watch the nude casino across or the powdered ladies on the side. One such night, it was only Alex and myself and I poured my heart out to him. He just couldn't relate to it. To his credit, neither did he feign understanding nor did he mock me.

'Mate, it's important that you structure your thinking. To me, you seem to be all over the place. Look at me. I always approach everything in a structured manner, be it work or seducing a woman. And without being immodest, I can tell you that I am successful, in my own eyes and that's what matters,' he said, adding as an afterthought, 'True, I have my own issues that I need to address but I don't waste time thinking about that. I work towards them or in my mind, I allot a time when I will work on them. You have to learn to compartmentalise various parts of your life. You can't allow one thread of abstraction to take over all other issues.'

'Issues?'

'Like I understand your issues to advise you on how to compartmentalise! You are just mind-fucking yourself, I say.' He blew a bubble out of his cigarette. I had always wanted to do that and I envied him.

'No, I meant your issues, like what?'

'Oh, that. I don't know, man. I guess you could put it down to my heritage, you know. I moved out of Greece at thirteen. Grew up in Australia. My parents separated when I was sixteen. My father went back to Greece while I stayed with my mum in Sydney. But I am as much an Australian as I am a fucking monkey. In fact, I have always tried hard to disassociate myself from Australia, my accent and everything. And it's not just Australia. I have problems attaching myself to anything. I have a commitment phobia. No, strike that out. I am a bloody nomad. The question of commitment doesn't even arise. And by commitment, I don't mean relationships, etc. I mean everything, from committing to a place to committing to a company to committing to even a friendship.'

I smiled. 'You sound as lost as I do, although on different things.'

'No. I am not. Currently, I have parked it under 'To do' but I will surely come back and sort it out. For the time being, I want to ensure that I do well at my job and get a confirmation. One thing at a time, mate.'

I considered his argument and queried, 'But how do you do that? I mean if this is as big a thing as you are making it out to be, then surely it would creep back from under the surface and the longer you avoid it, the more it will start affecting you and your job.'

'Well, you are partly right. But why do you see your job as disparate from your life? The success at your job would eventually allow you to explore the important things in your life. Besides, it's not like I have left it unattended. I kind of have an idea how to tackle it. It may mean that I need to go back to Greece, spend some time there and get an identity. Heh Heh, how vulgar does that sound now? And I thought, you were ostentatious earlier.' He laughed in an apologetic manner, 'Anyway, the thing is that once you have parked it with a promise to tackle it later, and not just an empty promise, after all you can't fool yourself, then it will not bother you or your job. In fact, you start to look at your job as a means to achieving the bigger end. For example, my boss has already promised me that if I do well, he would move me to a short-term assignment in Greece. It makes me even more focused now. You should do the same.'

'But really, if you want to move to Greece, aren't you simply wasting time here? I mean you could go back and find a job there on your own. Can't you?' I asked.

'There you go again – looking at only one side of the coin. Of course, I want to find my roots. But I also want other things in life; a plush job and a high-flying career, for example. So, I am trying my best to marry both.'

'Makes sense.'

That night, I had a dream that I had compartmentalised my feelings in my brain and then I couldn't find them anywhere. I felt naked to the bone and shamefully realised that I derived a sense of importance from that very disquiet. It seemed intuitive that I was in no way different or unique from others in any worldly sense and so I was trying to derive authenticity in the metaphysical sense. I woke up covered in sweat and I was perplexed if this was indeed true and if yes, how shallow I was.

Each one of us had figured out different ways of surviving. Alex was swimming. I was drifting. Dev was barely afloat while Arjuna was thinking of jumping the ship.

12

The Honeymoon is Over

It was just a matter of time before my 'playful inactivity' at office was noted. Even my best efforts at maintaining a busy exterior could not extend my period of paid unemployment. I was forced to submit the spreadsheet model and I was tasked with deploying it in Southeast Asia as the test market. The biggest part of the second leg of my project was to travel to various countries and conduct training on the use of the model. I instinctively disliked it, because I had to speak in front of a room full of people and there was no way of hiding one's incompetence.

Over time, I classified my audience into three groups. This helped me in deciding the best way to answer their questions. The first group consisted of those who were new in their jobs. They thought that they were smart, except they were not. They were a lethal combination of arrogance and absurdity, who asked mostly irrelevant and some downright dumb questions. I would arrogantly brush aside their doubts to the point of shattering their confidence and thus avoid follow-up questions. It helped that in most of these places, I introduced myself as a director or a manager or took on some such senior designation, revelling in the accompanying awe. At one such venue, when somebody asked me how I managed to rise so fast, I answered that it was because my uncle owned five per cent of the company stocks. The second group consisted of those who had been around for a while. They were either sufficiently numbed or were smart enough to realise the miniscule impact they could make on any project. This group, therefore, stayed quiet for the most part. I loved them and even bought them drinks after the day was over. The third group consisted of a minority of employees who had been doing very well, in line with their ambitions. They took every meeting as an opportunity to show how smart they were. In their mind, the only way they could do so was to find faults with others. Once the lie about my high position was added in the mix, they would sit up and ask tough questions so as to impress me, probably hoping that I would remember all this and one day, promote them. I hated this group.

This part of my training came with abundant travelling, of course. Initially, I welcomed the change in lifestyle and looked forward to it. I reasoned that it would keep me busy as I would be exposed to new places, people and cultures which should keep my mind materially focused, for a while, at least. However, it was not to be the case as I realised that most of my travelling was extremely frantic and my exposure limited to airports to hotels to offices to airports, punctuated by the lethally boring training sessions. Often I would take an early morning flight, retrace my steps late at night only to catch another flight the next morning. Initially, I loved the hospitality of the in-flight crew, how they addressed me as 'Mr Achet', as they bowed impossibly low, the in-flight entertainment, the wine and the dessert. But soon, I started asking them to just give me a blanket and a 'Do-not-disturb' sign. I longed for sleep but almost all the time, I would subscribe to the entertainment menu. I would watch the same movie over and over again, as my travelling was too frequent for the monthly upgrade of the movies schedules. On the rare occasions when I did sleep in-flight, I wouldn't be able to sleep after I arrived home. I spent so much time in airport terminals, in the air and in hotels that I was never sure of my bearings. There was a particular week in which I crossed borders five times and by the end of the week, I was not even sure which country I was in. My wallet was stuffed with different currencies and my passport was becoming increasingly dirty with red and blue stamps. I resigned myself to the situation, tried to be constructive and spent my time alternately working or penning down my thoughts.

Sometimes, I would cross the others, who were also now required to travel on their projects. On one such occasion, I happened to be in Bangkok along with Dev and Alex. It was a Friday and we extended our stay by one more night so we could witness Friday nightlife. Dev was keen to visit the colourful Patpong area and watch a bit of the ping-pong shows. But the majority vote won and we decided to keep it clean, and bounced from one pub to another. By the end of the night, we were walking in a stupefied, intoxicated manner. Alex, true to his reputation, had corned a beautiful Thai girl with whom he communicated alternately with lewd gestures of his hands and by kissing her. We had to cut his fun short since we were all sharing one hotel room to keep the cost down. He wasn't very happy. 'Come on, guys. I wouldn't have taken more than an hour. You could have waited outside for that time.'

Dev had replied, 'We would have, if you were hitching with a girl, mate. But that was a fucking trannie. You should actually be thankful to us.'

Alex was genuinely astonished. 'A trannie? That can't be a trannie. No way. Are you sure?'

'Yes, mate. Tell him, Achet.'

I hadn't noticed this anomaly and didn't feel like lying. 'I don't know, man. But now that you mention it, it did look a bit dodgy to begin with.'

'Exactly,' Dev continued, 'When in doubt, quit.'

'Fuck me. I feel so fucked right now. Do me a favour, don't mention this to anybody.' Alex made signs indicating kissing and groping. 'You know....all that.'

'We can speak and understand English fairly well, mate,' Dev acted as if he was offended.

'Sorry. But you know what I mean,' Alex said and started laughing. We all did. We laughed at the impossibility of the situation; three of us, away from home, on vague projects that we couldn't care less about, and in a strange country where the preferred language was that of gestures and where boys were more beautiful than girls. In between spitting, Dev said, 'If only I could get some grass around here.' No sooner had he mentioned it that it became a burning mission for all of us. In our liquor-infused brains, we childishly thought that in this world where nothing was going our way, it was only fair that we should get some cannabis at least. A desperate search ensued, without any worry about the consequences. First, we went to the guard house at the hotel and asked them if they could arrange for some grass. We were given some real hostile looks. Needless to say, it didn't work. We walked for about twenty minutes till we reached a cab-stand and asked a few guys there if they could help us. A helpful fellow junkie pointed us to a group of trishaws known locally as the 'Tuk-tuks.' As we walked towards them, it was three o'clock in the morning and the effect of alcohol was wearing off. We started noticing the smaller things like the mean faces around us, a pocketknife dangling by the side of a particularly tough guy, the smell of marijuana in the air and an unconscious girl lying by the side of the street. Alex's mumbled suggestion, 'Perhaps, we should just go home', was summarily dismissed by Dev as he stepped boldly in front, 'Hey you, any weed?' At first, they were incredulous. When they realised that we were asking for just about enough weed to make three joints, they started laughing at us. They took us through a small darkened alley to a clearing behind the main road and opened a large wooden crate which contained dried and powdered cannabis compressed into one big cake. There were at least a dozen or so such crates lying around. Alex was the first one to realise what we had walked into. He started apologising and asked them to let us go. They did but not before giving us a small cannabis-cake, the size of a matchbox, free.

After that brief scare, we sat down by the footpath figuring out where to smoke up. By now, Alex had sobered up and he declared that he didn't want to smoke up anymore. I suggested, 'Why don't we smoke up here itself'? but Dev put his foot down, 'We ought to smoke decently. Let's do that at the hotel room. We will be checking out by the morning anyway.' Nobody disagreed and soon, we sat on the comfortable sofa looking out of the window at the

Bangkok skyline. We were half-way through the joints when my phone rang. It was Arjuna. I was in a petty mood and so I asked Dev to answer it while putting it on speaker.

'Hello.'

Arjuna's voice came booming over. He seemed hassled, 'Is that Achet?'

'No.'

'Who is this?' He sounded baffled as he couldn't understand why somebody else would answer my phone. 'Could I speak to Achet?'

Dev continued messing with him. 'One question at a time, please.'

'Who is this?' After a moment's hesitation, he added, 'Dev?'

'One question at a time, please,' Dev repeated himself. Alex started rolling on the bed unable to contain his laughter.

'Fuck you, man. I need some urgent help here.' Arjuna was now extremely frustrated.

'You need help in fucking me? Should I bend over?'

'Just listen to me, okay…' But he was cut off by Dev. 'How can I listen to you if you keep on talking?'

'Huh?'

'Exactly.'

Now, it was my turn to fall on the floor. Dev couldn't keep a straight face any more either and we laughed like maniacs. Arjuna, by now, understood that we were all together and said in a serious voice, 'Guys, I am sitting in a cell. This is the one phone call allowed. Is there anybody sober down there?' It fell on deaf ears.

I asked, 'Why are you sitting in a cell?'

Arjuna replied, 'That isn't important. Right now, I need somebody to bail me out.'

'First, we have to understand whether we are bailing out a minor shoplifter or a psychopathic murderer.' More laughter ensued.

'Serious guys, please.' Alex, by now, sensed the urgency and took over the phone as the two of us continued rolling on the carpet. Next morning, he explained to us how Arjuna had been found in the company of a known terrorist from the LTTE and had been packed off to jail. Arjuna had claimed innocence and complete ignorance of his companion's background. Alex had to seek the company human resources manager's help in bailing Arjuna out. At Alex's suggestion, we had decided to confront Arjuna and ask him what was really going on.

'It's no big deal. He was trying to recruit me for some analytical stuff,' Arjuna said.

Alex asked, 'How do you know this guy?'

'My friend put me in touch with him. He said that it would be nothing more than just a chat. To be honest, I also wanted to find out about all possible ways that I could help the cause. It was pure bad luck that this guy's name was on Interpol's list and they tracked him down at precisely the same time.'

Dev said, 'Dude, you surely realise that terrorism is not the best way here. You are smart and intelligent enough to know that. Right?'

'Really? So when you guys were fighting for your independence, that was not terrorism?' Arjuna countered. 'In fact, it was probably described as terrorism by the government media back then. If you were born in that era, would you have disassociated yourself from the so-called terrorism and let your country be ruled by those who didn't care about it?'

Dev looked helpless. Alex took over. 'Mate, if it is purely a matter of finding out the various ways in which your people are fighting for their independence, it is fine. But really, think about it. You can help your cause in a more acceptable manner. Violence is not the best way.'

'I don't know, man. But it is still an option for me,' Arjuna said.

We realised that Arjuna was not going to be persuaded, and we gave up. He was bent upon trying to do something. His argument was valid too and hence, I had refrained from saying anything.

My stay in Singapore was coming to an end. A fast-paced lifestyle, coupled with a busy travelling schedule, had taken its toll on me. I went through a brief period when my memory was interspersed with spots, black and grey and blank. I was deprived of sleep and I was increasingly abusing anti-depressants. Those capsules helped calm me down but they greatly added to my memory decay. When I was not popping pills, I was smoking weed. My brain was at a complete loss to organise events in a suitable manner, conducive for easy recall. The events ran into each other and were so densely juxtaposed that my own life was becoming more like a jigsaw puzzle for me, a puzzle that neither interested me nor did I have enough energy to unlock its hidden meaning. At times, I would recall an event that happened days before and I would wonder if it did really happen and at other times, I could not recall what happened the night before, even if my life depended upon it. Some afternoons, I would have a nagging feeling that I was forgetting something and would rake my mind for clues, like an interrogator questioning a mute prisoner. I would then be forced to spend the entire day on a false trail and in the process, I would develop a severe migraine.

Then again, it wasn't necessarily depressing all this while. I grew increasingly closer to Dev, Arjuna, Bala and Alex. We were all grappling with problems of our own. Some were tangible while others were intangible. Alex's and Dev's sole focus was on doing well in their respective projects. Alex's motive was to generate adequate leverage so as to move to Greece with a plush job. Dev, on the other hand, was working hard to convert this opportunity of a lifetime into a successful career launch-pad. Although, he maintained that his project was an obvious attempt by the company to simply keep him busy, he still persisted in his attempts to extract some life out of it. Arjuna didn't give a damn about his career and continued his pursuit of finding a meaningful way to contribute to the Tamil crusade. However, to his credit, like Alex, he was able to switch off his mind from it and work hard when it mattered. Bala was fairly successful in her career but oscillated dangerously between her wild lifestyle and some subconscious womanly urge to stabilise her life by marrying a 'nice boy.' As we wrestled with our problems, we became extremely supportive of each other. I would have to say that the time spent with them was probably the best time during my entire trip. These guys were loyal and never judged me for my faults, while always reinforcing my strengths. I also helped them out where I could. Inadvertently, we started resembling a clan; one that was firmly forged with friendship, one that was greatly admired by outsiders and at the same time, one that dispelled unwanted outsiders.

The side effect was that I was increasingly succumbing to social isolation and feeling proud of the same.

The other good part was my work. In spite of my active efforts at ridiculing corporate life and making a mockery of the passionate way my superiors and peers took to an otherwise trivial job in the larger cosmic scheme, I was still able to get by. I got a decent appraisal on my first project. It was around this time that I was sent on the second leg of training to Malaysia. I didn't mind it. Honestly, Singapore was turning out to be extremely dismal and phoney. Almost everybody was highly material, to the point of being obnoxious. It was as if they inhabited human bodies which were hollowed inside out, as if famished termites had consumed all the substance. Immorality abounded, and behind the façade of high society, there was a dangerous animal taking over. I had felt threatened as I was increasingly drawn towards nightly drinking orgies, even though it had started at first as an escape from my riotous anxiety. I felt that I could do with some time alone and so I welcomed the move to Malaysia. I was sad to leave my friends behind but I was secretly happy to have escaped with minor injuries. Nonetheless, before moving on to Malaysia, I asked for a week off, having thought up a by-pass surgery on my father. My boss reluctantly agreed. I wasn't sure why I wanted to go home or anywhere for that matter, but it was almost subconsciously imperative that I did. Perhaps I wanted to get rid of the dependence on the anti-depressants and I felt I could only do that on home ground. Perhaps I was feeling guilty for losing sight of my family and wanted to assuage that guilt. Perhaps I needed to relive my provincial life, even if for just a few days, to reconcile with my current life. Perhaps I was seeking an 'identity' under the influence of Alex. Who knew? Whatever be the case, I found myself back at the house with blue hostile walls and reluctant, translucent windows.

While we were brought together by similar circumstances, our friendship was, in reality, forged by the undercurrent of our troubles, however dissimilar. Ironically, those very same troubles were now working towards pulling us apart. Increasingly, we were becoming too absorbed in ourselves and our own little problems. The thought of listening to others and their troubles had started to require too much effort, almost to the point of being unbearable. Without lying, I could say that I suffered from this selfish trait and that others did, too.

13

Stranger at Home

WITHIN THE FIRST couple of days of my stay at my home, I was already feeling the monotony. I was a stranger in my own house. When I looked into the mirror, an unfamiliar face looked back accusingly. I would wake up late in the mornings. Sometimes, I slept till noon. That, in itself, was good enough reason for insomnia at night. Coupled with the fact that I had discarded the sleeping tablets, it ensured that my sleeping cycle was effectively ruined. I would go through the day as if I was doing a giant favour to the universe. I would try to read a book but wouldn't get past the first few paragraphs. I would try my hand at the crossword puzzle, only to be annoyed to the point of tearing my hair out, as I found myself incapable of solving simple clues which I could have solved in my sleep at one point of time. When my mother asked me if there was something wrong, I simply shook my head. My conversations with my parents could only be described at best as 'small talk.' We mostly talked about the weather. The only time we spent together would be at the dinner table. Thankfully, it was a long-established habit of eating in front of the television and that precluded any real conversation. I purposefully avoided the living room at other times so as to minimise my interaction with them. Throughout this period, I didn't call my school friends or even Radha, even though one of the reasons I came here was to apologise to her and to get a formal closure. I didn't know what I would say to them. I was so agitated that I decided to cut my stay short by making up another story about how I was needed badly at the office. But on the evening I was to leave, I started feeling anxious yet again and I dreaded leaving, so muddled was my mind. I came out and stood at the compound wall to observe the empty street ahead that had calmed me so many times in the past.

'I heard you leaving the house in the dead of night, last night.' My father came out to join me. His words could have been accusing but the tone was friendly.

'Yeah.' I debated whether I needed to offer an explanation after all these years. It seems some basic values had survived, like respect for elders, and so I added, 'I was not sleepy so I went for a walk.'

'It's funny. In your entire statement, the pause was the most eloquent.' He stood next to me leaning over the wall. The scene was the same as was etched in my memory pane albeit set in the evening; the semi-deserted street in front, the leafless tree on the left and the lifeless façade of a school on the right. The only missing part was my father on his loud scooter for he was standing next to me. 'You know why we construct these walls?'

'Is this one of your trick questions?' I asked.

I probably need to talk about my father a bit here. He was the eldest of three brothers and four sisters in a family headed by a fierce patriarch who somehow brought them all up from a small brokerage business. I had been told that my father had promise and he was set to become a lawyer, a feat bigger than one's dreams in those days. But something snapped somewhere and he came back home, having abandoned his pursuit. Nobody ever talked about it and it was silently understood to be a taboo topic. Since then, he had lived his entire life under the shadow of his father who, for some reason would never trust him with anything. Even the accounting entries that my father would put down on the rare occasions when my grandpa was indisposed, would be checked and corrected a thousand times. With each correction, my father would be duly admonished and forbidden from ever touching the ledger again. I could never understand why my father never retaliated but that's how it was. He spent this part of his life performing his mediocre duties as diligently as he could and now, he helped my grandpa in getting through the daily routine of his incapacitated life, probably still waiting for that elusive reconciliation.

'Come on. Play along,' my father said.

'To keep unwanted elements at bay?' I tried to humour the old man while keeping my irritation hidden.

'And to keep the desired elements within.' He looked at me and I noticed those twinkling eyes amid grey beard and a full head, yet again. 'The trick is to know which is which.'

'Sorry, you lost me at the last statement.' I was getting drawn into the conversation yet again. Just like the old times when he used to draw me in as a kid into the over-related story about the old parrot who coughed. The old man hadn't lost his touch.

'Do you know who should be inside those walls that you have

built up so closely around you? Is there anybody in there at all?' He lifted a big ant from the top of the wall and carefully placed it on the ground, in the process exerting his back and letting out a slight sigh.

'I don't have any walls around me, Papaji. Don't be overly dramatic. You seem to be watching too many soap operas off late.' I was caught in the tussle of whether to entertain him and regret it later or to brush him aside and regret it now.

'Maybe. In old age, you become wise or you become childish or if you are really wise, you are wise at times and childish at others.' He was staring straight ahead into the empty street, his weight supported on his elbows perched atop the yellow wall which was covered intermittently with bird droppings. 'Your grandpa used to say that if you say something wise, chances are that people will make you believe that it is childish because they can't face the truly wise.'

'What did he say about old men being base?' I hoped that he would catch the sarcasm in my statement. A cart selling ice cream was coming laboriously into view. It reminded me of the time when grandpa used to give us fifty paise each, for an orange bar.

The thought must have crossed my father's mind as well for he was checking his pockets for loose change, 'Do you want an ice cream?'

'Sure.'

'Your grandpa said that old men should know well enough to be sufficiently childish or else risk a very lonely life indeed.'

'How is that?'

'When you are childish, people around you pity you and thereby take care of you. If you are wise all the time, people are eventually going to become sick of you because they don't like to be told what to do all the time.'

'I guess that last bit is applicable to all and not just old men?'

Papaji smiled while looking at his thick and grimy toenail. 'It is. However, a young mind won't realise it till after some time, because the young live under the presumption that they can take care of themselves and thus, they try to be wise all the time. And herein lies the paradox since that very assumption makes them immature but in a way that is neither pitiable nor curable.'

'So you think I suffer from that trait?'

'No more than I suffered from it in my younger days.'

'Then what's the point? Time is the only cure. Isn't it?'

'I don't know, beta. I am telling you all this so that you don't make the same mistakes as I did or at least, you recover before it's too late. It looks like I have failed miserably. I should stick to being childish.' Wearily, he hailed the ice-cream cart to come over to our gate.

I didn't need to say it. I really shouldn't have said it. But I said it anyway. 'Just because you were too late doesn't mean that everybody is going to do the same. Is that why grandpa and you are not on speaking terms? You probably deserved it.'

I could sense his distress, even though it was not visible. He muttered, 'If you don't know enough, then you ought to hold your tongue.' He made to move back inside the house, his hunch more pronounced than before. But he stopped midway, came back and stood in the same position for some time before whispering, more to himself than to me, 'You are probably right. I was too late and too stubborn.'

'Orange-bar again, chotte bhaiya?' The ice-cream vendor, popularly known as 'ice cream wala bhaiya' in the colony, enquired.

'Make that two, and large as well. I am paying.' Papaji beckoned.

Two dripping orange bars hastily appeared in the lined and work-hardened hands of the ice-cream wala bhaiya. They created a dripping trail on the dried sand as they made their way to us. Papaji paid with both cash and words and we started licking the bars.

While departing, the man hollered, 'Chotte bhaiya, you have come after a long time. You should keep coming home more often. It is good to see you having the orange bar, just like old times.'

'Tastes good,' asked my father.

I replied, 'The same as always.'

He glanced at me and smiled to himself. 'I remember, you used to really love these moments. If it was an orange bar, it would be described as the best orange bar yet. If it was *bhelpuri*, it would have been the best experience your taste buds would have ever received.'

'Things change.'

'Yes. They do. Remember the parrot story? How you always asked me to narrate the same story every night, even though you knew it by heart and you would actually correct me on even the smallest omissions in narration, here and there?'

I was finding this conversation a little embarrassing, so I quipped, 'Papaji, don't you think I am a little too old for it now?'

I saw the eyebrow rise again as his eyes looked straight into mine, giving me the sensation of being bared to the bone. 'Actually,

I think you are just about old enough for it now. Ever wondered why the parrot coughed all night?'

'Yeah. To keep the cat away from his clan.'

'And still it was his own clan that banished him for creating too much noise. And they paid for it when the cat ate them all.'

'Not all of them. Didn't the survivors realise their mistake and get the old parrot back?'

He smiled again without looking at me, like it was a small triumph for him. 'Yes. They did. I was wondering if you would correct me again. At least there was something that I was able to ingrain in you properly.'

'You are sounding a bit strange today. Where are you going with all this?'

'I didn't make up that story. It was and is real. The old parrot is nobody else but your grandpa. He barks but only because he cares. I was the one who almost drove him away but I realised my mistake…though a touch too late.'

I reckoned silence was the most appropriate response. He continued, ensuring he looked into nothingness in the street ahead. I couldn't tell if his eyes were moist. 'You see, back in the day, I was a confident young man and was reaching for the skies. I went for higher studies and joined the 'classier' people. I was embarrassed to be seen with my family. When my sister visited me, I acted like I was a stranger offering charity to an orphan. She left feeling bad and my father got to know about it. When I went back for money to fund my education (which was only a pretext for I really wanted to fund my excesses), he showed me the door. I vowed never to return and in my fury, I said things that I shouldn't have said. But I did recover and came back before I was lost forever.'

'What made you come back?'

'I can't tell you that. Besides it was not one incident but a series of events which led to this realisation. Everybody has to make this journey on his own. If you grow up in a glasshouse, you are doomed to be somebody's dinner.'

A group of children came to the park on the left for a game of cricket followed by elderly people on their leisurely evening walk. I noticed the absence of people from my age group. I was surprised when I realised that it had always been the case, even though I never really bothered with this small detail before. I wondered where we hid during these serene times; did we ever come out at any point of time? And almost immediately I knew that we were the uneasy creatures of the night. We would never risk exposure to the rest of the world for we were too wise. So, the only way we could find our way was to run into obstacles and take corrective measures for that which we couldn't see.

As my father made to move back inside, I instinctively asked, 'Why was I named Achet?'

'Oh. You don't know?' I shook my head. He continued, 'When you were born, you didn't cry at all. We were afraid whether you were stillborn especially since it was a premature delivery. And then suddenly, you cried out. So your Grandpa named you Achet – the one who has been asleep for long.' He paused and then added, 'It was the loveliest sound we ever heard. Your grandpa prophesied then that you would do wonderful things the day you wake up.'

'The day I wake up?'

'Yes. The day you wake up.' He winked.

I was fortunate to have this conversation. Although I missed the entirety of the message, it did put things into perspective for me. I made up my mind to move from a life of indulgence to one of abstinence. The truth was that it didn't really matter.

◆

14

Abstinence

KUALA LUMPUR WAS truly the first place I arrived in, without knowing anybody. I found the experience to be quite enriching, to say the least. There was relatively more chaos here than in Singapore but not so much so as to make it unbearable. It was the right mix between an Indian metropolis and Singapore, and I liked it that way. I was put up in a service apartment and this time I had the whole apartment to myself. Further, I was also provided with a rented car, but that was a little later. One of my first bizarre experiences was while dealing with local cabs, as the rented car wasn't due for another week or so. During that week, I called up cabs whenever I had to go anywhere. On my very first day, I located a call-a-cab number in the telephone directory and asked for a cab. The operator rudely asked, 'Wherefrom and whereto' to which I dutifully gave my apartment address and the office address. She said, 'Okay, bye,' and hung up. Not sure, I called them up again and was greeted by a different operator, albeit in the same rude tone. I complained that the previous operator hung up on me, which fell on deaf ears. The rest of the conversation was an exact repeat of the previous one and she also hung up with the ominous words 'Okay, bye.' I was wondering what was going on. I was running late and I had not foreseen this complication. Shortly, I got a call from the first operator who told me that a cab was on its way. I was relieved and proceeded to the office. Midway to the office, about twenty minutes later, I got a call from the second operator who told me that the cab is outside the lobby and that I had better get my ass down there. I tried to explain the confusion but realised that she was in no mood to listen. I panicked and switched off my phone.

For the first few days, my entertainment sources were similar in kind. I took it to the next level on lazy weekend afternoons when I would call up the cab companies on purpose, to drive them nuts. I would make false calls, provide weird addresses and then I would lean back and enjoy as the operator would get increasingly frustrated. I had realised that they didn't carry detailed database of their customers and thus they could not blacklist anybody even if they wanted to. Those were my small 'trips' during an otherwise fairly solitary and peaceful stay.

The Malaysian office was mostly staffed with people who had been married to this company for years and weren't really in the same age group as me. Nonetheless, they invited me to their social gatherings wherein I mostly played the part of a baby-sitter as they beat the same topics to death; topics ranging from their salary levels, office gossips, local politics revolving around the sodomy accusation against a prominent leader, and other such petty issues. On rare occasions, I was also invited to family gatherings of the local Indian expatriate group where discussions mostly centred on reminiscing about India, against the background score of Bollywood music. I would cynically muse that if these people loved India so much, then why would they come all the way out here? It wasn't like there was a dearth of good, paying jobs in India, not in this age of humungous growth that the country was witnessing. I attended these gatherings only because of lack of anything better to do. Besides, having managed to stay off anti-depressants ever since my Jaipur trip, I was afraid that I might lapse back into the vicious cycles of depression, cannabis and pills if I cut myself off completely from the world.

My training over the course of two months was in the Sales department. I spent about a week in office after which I moved to the field, tailing a veteran salesman in order to learn the art of selling. His name was Zul. He was thirty-four years old, Muslim and a bachelor. He was short and round and sported a moustache and cropped hair. He was in charge of an area called 'Petaling Jaya' and had been so for seven years of his total service of nine years. In his own words, he was looking forward to his ten years' loyalty award due in another year. When I asked what the award was, he had replied proudly, 'a watch with the company name printed in gold'. He was two levels lower than the level I was hired at but he wasn't intimidated by that at all. He was passionately in love with his job and he even went to the extent of saying that he was born to sell.

I tailed Zul for two weeks, wherein we would go from one retail shop to another, take down orders from the shop-owners and then instruct the transporters, also known as merchandisers, to deliver the products. I found it to be an extremely tiring task as we would drive to a particular route and then cover the entire gamut of stores on foot; sometimes under the hot tropical sun and sometimes under a torrential downpour. When it rained for the first time we were out, I suggested we ought to come back later. Zul replied, 'Heaven or hell, a good salesman will not be deterred.' He would meticulously prepare in advance for each sales visit and ask me to observe everything closely if I wanted to become a good salesman like him. After each sale, he would pull me aside to ask me what I had learnt. The first time, I was caught off-guard. Somehow, I managed to mumble that I admired his relationship with the shop-owner. He was sufficiently pleased and proceeded to give me an entire lecture on how he knew each shop-owner personally. He, apparently, knew even the names of their kids. I reckoned that it was possible only because of years of regular visits and lack of any personal life outside work. Although, I didn't think I would be bothered with the names of the shop-owners' kids, whether I did the same job for nine years or ninety years. In the next store, however, he was summarily dismissed by the shop-owner like one would dismiss a persistent beggar. I mercifully avoided commenting on that.

At the end of the first day of sales training, he took me to a roadside café, also known as 'Mamak' in the local lingo, and ordered *roti-canai* for both of us. This would become our daily routine. When I objected to the unhealthy looking curry, he responded, 'Now you a salesman, eh? So you eat like one. A salesman has curry and such crap, like sailorman.' He was so overbearing that I didn't bother with further objections. Mamak shops were a cultural phenomenon in Malaysia and you could find them anywhere. Most of them were open till late and some even claimed to be open round-the-clock. Whether it was lunchtime or dinnertime, afternoon or 4 a.m. in the morning, you would find them busy serving customers. The service was appalling and it reminded me of the bars in a western movie. One of their prime selling points was often a television set tuned to the latest soccer game. Some even had projector screens. Somehow, the soccer game seemed to unify a seemingly disparate set of customers. The food served was authentic local food. It was mostly good, always allowing for a tiny bit of uncertainty. Sometimes, you would feel lucky when it turned out to be absolutely delicious. On rare occasions, you would have an immediate urge to visit the toilet in the rear. Once, my day was made when I couldn't find any toilet paper. Fortunately, these shops were devoid of sleaze and concerned themselves only with food and soccer.

As we were drinking, Zul suddenly ducked below the table. I thought this was also one of those salesmen's customs and so I did the same. I observed from under the table, 'It certainly is cosy down here.' Apparently, he had noticed somebody familiar and he didn't want to be spotted. He explained, 'Creditors,' I felt sorry for him and concocted a story about how I owed a lot of money for my education too, and how I could totally empathise with him. He suddenly warmed to me. With more outings, he opened up even more. When I asked him the reason for being a bachelor, he pleasantly surprised me with his reply, 'My salary not enough lah. I run an orphanage with seventy-eight kids. It eats up all my earning. Hence the debts. But I am not complaining. That orphanage is my first love.'

I told him how I admired his life; consummate salesman by the day and a good samaritan by the night, and asked, 'I can understand your passion about this orphanage but how can you remain so passionate about this sales job?'

'See, I myself grew up in an orphanage. Not recommended at all.' Laughing, he continued, 'So, I wanted to establish something that the kids could think of as a real home. Isn't it some Indian who said that change should start from you or something like that?'

I supplied him Gandhi's name.

'Yes. Yes. That's the guy. But not easy to run an orphanage, you know. Needs money. Our company has this policy of matching any employee spending that goes to a not-for-profit venture. So, I spend as much money as possible on this orphanage to maximise the company contribution,' He winked. 'Now you know why I am single.'

I continued my query, 'But still so much enthusiasm for selling?'

'Are you stupid or something? Didn't you hear what I just said? My company helps me so much in running this orphanage. They even get me sponsorships. My colleagues even volunteer to teach these kids for free. Of course, I will do my job to the best of my capabilities. I can't let them down, no?'

Zul continued asking me what I had learnt after every sales trip, for the entire duration. Soon, I ran into a problem as I had exhausted narrating all the possible sales tips I could pick up. I hinted that my training was over but he didn't get it and persisted with those debrief meetings. My creativity reserves failed me and I resorted to falling back on admiring his relationship with the retailers. I used this line in succession for quite a few debrief sessions. He liked the flattery for some time but in the end, he lost it. 'What you repeat all the time? Relationship, relationship! Come on, these shop-owners solid businessmen. They don't buy 'cause I am their son-in-law. Give me something more. Didn't you see the discount I offered?' That night, Zul appeared in my nightmare and demanded a twenty-page report on the sales training.

All in all, however, I liked Zul. He didn't complain; not about the dullness of his job of so many years, not about the gap between his salary and his expenses, not about the lack of attention from his trainee. He actually went out of his way to make the most of what he had and he was genuinely happy in his pursuits. He was diagonally my opposite. He sought meaning in the pursuit of happiness while I tried to find happiness in the pursuit of meaning. I liked him precisely because he was so different from me. At the end of the training, I thanked him sincerely for his efforts. I promised to keep in touch with him, knowing that I wouldn't keep the promise.

I considered Zul a prime example of how inspiration could spring from the least expected direction. He also seeded a thought that the company was really no different from the people who worked in it. Some were good, some were bad but the worst culprits were insider moles like me.

15

To Each His Own

THE OTHERS WERE in sporadic contact with me via e-mail and phone. Dev was given yet another project but he maintained that it was yet another useless project, probably even more so than the previous one. He said that at this rate, they would likely fail him and he would be back where he started. He mentioned all this in a mocking tone, as if he couldn't care less. I wondered why he would write such things if he wasn't really concerned about them. It wasn't as if he had many job offers in hand; then I selfishly decided: to each his own. One fine evening, he actually called me from office. After the exchange of pleasantries, he said, 'I know that I am not making it. So, I have decided that I am going to abuse company resources thoroughly. Do you know that in the past month or so, I have charged all my personal calls to the office? My friends in the US and UK who hadn't heard from me for a long time were surprised to get my calls. I would talk to them for hours. If they are going to give me the shaft, I am going to at least make the most of it. Savvy, eh?'

'Dude, why don't you focus on the project, and at least make something out of it? This is your only chance to make it in this company. Why are you ruining it? It is almost as if you yourself don't want to succeed.' It sounded very unlike me. But I thought my concern must have originated from my liking for Dev.

He complained, 'I have told you, mate. These are all dud projects. There is no point in wasting my time on this.'

'Firstly, I don't think it is a dud project and even if it was, it is not as if you are doing anything worthwhile with your free time. Calling up old acquaintances and thinking they are your friends when they haven't even bothered to stay in touch. Do they even talk to you for a minute, leave alone for hours, or are you making it all up?'

I visualised him considering my accusation. He decided to skirt it. 'Unsolicited advice goes unheeded, mate. If I need advice, I would ask for it. Anyhow, have you figured out how to get some marijuana in that godforsaken country?'

'Not really. I haven't had it for a long time now. I don't think I am addicted to it.'

'That's a shame. And I thought you were original. Anyhow, take care.' He hung up.

He never called me again but continued to drop sporadic e-mails, each one sounding more constructive than before. He mentioned that he was acting on my advice and was working hard on his project. He even talked about prospects of patching up with his girlfriend. However, those e-mails did not bear the mark of his customary enthusiasm and he seemed more resigned than ever. Although I pitied him, I couldn't bring myself to reply. I blamed it on the fact that his e-mails were almost always too absorbed with himself. Very rarely did he enquire about what was going on in my life. But the reality was that I was as self-absorbed, if not more, and I couldn't be bothered with his concerns. I never wrote back after that call.

Alex was doing extremely well. He had impressed his supervisor with his work and he was almost sure that he would be posted in Greece for his next assignment. I was happy for him. He was, however, a bit concerned about Arjuna and said, 'Mate, I have managed to get him out of his terrorist stunts. But he needs somebody around him constantly, to keep him in check. If I move off to Greece, then he could lapse. Could you promise me that you would keep in touch with him and make sure that he is alright?' I guardedly replied, 'I honestly don't know what the right thing is. How can I even begin to understand his evident passion, leave alone advise him about the right path? I don't know how you have managed to keep him in line so far. Hats off to you for that but I am not sure if I can do that.' In fact, I was dreading the responsibility. How could I bring myself to look after somebody else when I myself needed looking after?

Arjuna, on the other hand, wasn't doing too well with his project. He had started working on a radio show for 'curry' immigrants in Singapore, something similar to what he had done in Melbourne. He was really excited about that. Alex had obviously influenced him towards a different way of working for his race. I was convinced that it did affect his performance and when I casually asked him about it, he shouted, 'You Indians don't understand the concept of life from an Aussie standpoint. You are all hungry little idiots and for you, success is to be at the top and everything else is a failure. I mean, Dev wouldn't settle for anything less than to be the fucking CEO of this company. I am not built like that. I don't want to go all the way up there. I am not that ambitious. I want to live a moderate life, a balanced life. I thought you were more like me, come on now, Achet.' I then apologised to him.

All these conversations weren't really initiated by me; everybody concerned themselves with their lives only and from the looks of it, they didn't even bother to listen to the other's point of view. Sometimes, I felt I needed somebody to listen to me but I had noticed the alarming lack of interest from others. Besides, I realised that firstly, I wouldn't even be able to articulate what I wanted to say, and secondly, I couldn't possibly expect anybody to relate to it. I didn't blame them for it. After all, I myself couldn't quite understand why Dev would not simply put his head down and ensure that his job got confirmed or how Arjuna could be so passionate about a struggle thousands of miles away from where he was. Nonetheless, I came to consider such conversations with others as welcome intrusions in an otherwise self-centred, condemnatory view of the world.

Still, I had a maddeningly large amount of free time in the evenings and looked for ways to spend it. I sought out an online community which organised weekend get-togethers. Most such gatherings were attended by expatriates. Some of those 'expatriates', for all practical reasons, were now residing in Malaysia for good but still kept themselves far removed from the locals and looked down at them. These communities also included some Indians who had developed strange accents. They would proudly complain that the locals could not understand them. I also spotted a few white nomads who had decided to be in Malaysia purely because of the local women's fascination with white skin. They didn't have a proper job and took up ad hoc assignments here and there while their girlfriends fed them. The only odd element was the women who joined such outings, for they were successful, local, Chinese women. Initially, I thought that they were obsessed with Caucasians and their motive was to get laid. This turned out to be an oversimplification. These women were actually educated abroad and now they found it difficult to gel with the local community. This was, thus, their way of seeking an 'abroad away from abroad'.

After attending a few such gatherings, I discarded them in favour of quieter evenings at Mamak shops. I considered myself quite at home there and almost felt part of the community. Sometimes, when I was lucky, I would have a guileless conversation with a simple local. Most of the time, however, I would just sit by myself and observe folks, some relaxed and some rushed, who would come to have their dinner, pay their dues and leave. It was so similar to the Jaipur railway station where I would sit for hours as a young boy. I had stumbled upon that scene when I was angry at my mother for not saving some of my favourite food for me. I had decided to run away and show them that I 'meant business'. I had sat there for a few hours before I was traced but in those few hours, I had observed and seen a lot. I had witnessed ecstatic welcomes and tearful farewells. I had also noted the cynical eyes of a passenger, an outsider who had gotten off a train to get a cup of tea, as he silently ridiculed what he saw. He had fascinated me. Perhaps that was the time I had decided that I would never be the one to welcome anybody nor would I be the one to bid goodbye. I had decided that I would be the one that others would welcome or see off. I had irrevocably condemned myself to be an eternal traveller. Sitting in the Mamak shop, I mused whether at that young age, I could have been capable of such deep thought but I was almost sure that it did have a bearing on my life that followed. I realised that the independent and important choice I had made had been my turning point. Earlier, I had thought that I was just following my brother's footsteps in moving out of Jaipur but now I was sure that it was entirely my decision.

When Bala told me that she was going to be in KL for a meeting and asked if I wanted to meet up for dinner, I had agreed nonchalantly. When the evening arrived, however, I realised that I was actually looking forward to it. I was so in love with the Mamak shop next to my apartment that I forced her to come eat there, despite her suspicions about the local food. On the whole, she didn't mind it. The waiter brought *roti canai* and a chai each.

Bala dipped her bread in the curry and held it in front of her face as she asked, 'Where did you get your hair from, mister? Underwent some hair weaving programme, did you?' My hair had not been violated by a pair of scissors for some time now and it showed.

'No. It was a hair transplant. Hair imported all the way from Greenland, forcibly taken from the body of a dead Eskimo, guaranteed to last,' I remarked and sipped some chai, 'All done in a humane and environmental-friendly manner, of course. They even have an ISO 9000 certificate. Or so the brochure claims. How is the food?'

Bala laughed out loud and a small bit of chewed bread travelled to and settled on my left shoulder, 'This food is nice.

Why would you need to apply force to take hair from a dead Eskimo's body?'

'Ha ha ha. Try pulling hair out of a body, dead or alive. It requires force, unless it is a wig, that is.'

'Ha ha ha. How come you are in such a frivolous mood today?' Bala asked.

'Been like that ever since my girlfriend dumped me,' I lied. On a separate note, I was slightly happy to have discovered my frivolous side again. Bala remarked, 'Looks like it was for the better.'

'It's always for the better. The cosmos have a customised plan for me, if not for everyone.' I felt luckier, found optimism hiding somewhere within, and tried my best to coerce it out.

'And what is that plan?'

'It could be a conspiracy or a fairytale. I am in the midst of uncovering it. It is a lifelong process, literally so.'

Bala turned serious and toyed with her cup of chai, 'I know what you mean.'

'Is something wrong?' I asked.

'No. Everything's fine.' She seemed indecisive. But I didn't want to push the matter any further and tried to change the topic, 'How was your meeting?'

'Actually, no, it's not fine.' She had made up her mind now. I found her frequent change of mind quite cute. She continued, 'I slept with Suraj.'

'Tell me more.'

'That's all. Isn't that bad enough? I mean, just a few months earlier, I had promised myself that I would not stray again anymore and that I would focus on finding Mr Right. And here I have done it again. And at such a time!'

'Sleeping with someone is not necessarily bad,' I said wearily. I wondred when Indians would free themselves of such social taboos.

'Yeah, yeah. I have heard all that before. I used to loudly advocate all that myself before.'

'You said something about the timing. What was that?'

'I am twenty-six now. It is about time I found a normal guy and settle down. I have been doing the rounds on the arranged marriage front. There is this guy with whom the talks have advanced a bit and there might have been a future.' She added, 'Now, I feel too dirty to continue with it. I feel I will be giving him a bad deal and he deserves better. I remembered your attack on Suraj's strange morality. I think I might have committed the same crime. If I go by what you say, I should stay away from him. Isn't it so?'

'First you need to ask yourself the question why you did it.'

'It isn't like I am dating this guy or anything. But there is something promising there. Now if he finds out about it, I am sure things will be stalled. '

'You didn't answer my question.'

She contemplated on the matter for a while before answering 'I don't know. I have...' She paused, 'needs. I was feeling lonely and needed somebody to comfort me, and Suraj was there. I wasn't sure if what I feel about this 'marriage guy' is love or just lust in operation and so, I have been rather guarded with him. It seems that there is something far greater at stake if I made any wrong moves with him. With Suraj, on the other hand, there were no repercussions involved, or so I thought. Besides, I don't really understand the arranged marriage concept. How can I be expected to suddenly fall in love with a complete stranger?'

The waiter cleared the plates. Bala waited till he had left. 'Don't you have anything to say?'

I decided to toe the fine line. 'Alex seems to think that the world runs on lust. I agree with him. I think love is at best just a choice. Love doesn't catch you unaware. You make a choice to love someone. It is neither true nor a compromise; it is a strong thread or a connection with another person that makes you earth-bound, by adding its own gravity. You need love because it is a way to justify your mortal life. Because, you are at least sure that there is someone in the thirteen billion light years of the universe whose primary concern is you. Otherwise, how would it matter whether you lived your life as a professional slut or a virgin bride? Not when the sixty or eighty years you grace this world for, is just the blink of an eye on the cosmic scale.' I had finished my chai and asked for another one. 'Have you seen the movie *Shall we dance*'? She shook her head. I continued, 'It is a rubbish movie but sometimes you find gold in rubbish. In the movie, Susan Sarandon is asked a question: why she married. She replies that she married because she needed a witness to her life. I found that to be a very thoughtful observation.'

'You said love is a choice and an easy one at that. What happens to people who don't make that choice?'

'I don't think all the people out there need love. While love is a strong connection with another individual, you can take the other route and form numerous, albeit weaker, connections with the masses. You can do it for example, if you are a celebrity, an actor, a humanitarian, a writer or a sportsman or in other similar fields. You develop a connection with a lot of people through your writings, acting, or athletic activity. This way, you have numerous, although uninvolved, witnesses to your life. Sometimes you may find that that is enough. But it is the harder of the two choices.'

'I am quite confused now. I don't know what I should do.'

'Why, it's simple really. You just have to make the choice. I don't think anything else will matter, once you have made that choice.'

I didn't realise till quite late in the day that this was all Bala needed to hear. Funnily enough, it seemed so straightforward and yet it had escaped her. To be honest, I myself completely missed the point when something similar had happened to me, and I had to pay a huge cost for it.

16

Mind is Restless

With the apprenticeship under Zul over, I was now given charge of five routes previously under him. I was to deliver a certain sales target by the end of the month, which would signal the end of my training stint in Kuala Lumpur. I also had a fixed budget to run promotions. My task consisted of three simple steps. First, to pay a daily visit to the stores on those routes in the morning and con the owners to place orders with me. Second, to ensure that the company products were properly visible on the shelf. The last one was to liaise with the logistics vendor, to deliver those orders by nightfall. Simple as it all sounded, I instinctively knew that I had a better chance of attaining Nirvana than to reach the sales target.

Having been with this company for some time now, I realised that I could still escape largely unhurt, as long as I had a good story to explain my failure. So, I spent the first morning at home, trying to list down reasons for my impending failure. Even this turned out to be quite a challenge. I started with listing the language barrier as the first excuse. I could say that most of these store-owners were either not able to speak English or they would simply not deal with somebody who didn't speak Malay. Under the merits of this excuse, I wrote that I would blame cultural insensitivity if my supervisor didn't believe me, since I was the only Indian salesman. The demerit was that I knew this in my mind to be only a partial truth, definitely not something that could stop an 'enterprising' salesman. Besides, there was the possibility of Zul contradicting me, saying that he had introduced me well enough to all the shop-owners. I thought about other excuses and realised that I had already run out of them. I thought harder and listed down the age-old, tried-and-tested sickness excuse. The beauty of this excuse was obviously that there was no getting past it. Unfortunately, it was a tad unbelievable.

For the life of me, I couldn't think of any other excuse and so I turned my attention to how I could sell, with the least amount of effort. I briefly wondered if I could buy the entire stock myself and destroy it but the numbers required me to be a millionaire. I further speculated if I could operate from home, that is, take the orders from the shop-owners over the phone and then pass it to the logistics assistant, again over the phone. It was likely that I would not meet the target but it was reasonable to assume that I would achieve a respectable sales level at least. I started to feel good and made it my fall-back option, even as I continued my search for better alternatives.

When no other brainwave occurred, I proceeded to go down the list of retail shops, and one by one, dialled their numbers to take down the order. Most refused to place an order over the phone to an unrecognisable voice. A few, however, did place an order, probably because they had run out of products and needed it badly. By the afternoon, I compiled a list of total orders. To my dismay, it was less than fifteen per cent of the required target for that day. Clearly, I needed to think of something drastic but I told myself that I would do it the next day. Presently, I called up the logistics agent and gave him the summary of the orders over phone. He responded, 'But you have to come down here, sir, for filing paperwork.' I explained to him the recent change in my company policy and that no documentation was required anymore, and that from now on, I would communicate with him only over the phone. 'But it's too small an order, sir. Not even the size of a mini-truck.' He had pointed out one anomaly I had forgotten to include in my careful considerations. I threw the question back at him. 'So what do we do now?' He ignored my question and instead asked in an understanding tone, 'You taking the orders on phone too, sir?' when I answered in the affirmative, he replied to the unasked question. 'Sir, you are not the first salesman to do so. But definitely the first with such small orders. Even I can do better than this. Anyway, I will see what I can do.'

I reckoned I had worked hard enough for the day to not be hassled by his caustic remarks. Suddenly, brilliance flashed through my brain and I realised that nothing prevented him from taking the orders for the next day as he delivered the stocks today. I estimated his salary based upon some Internet research. I figured that if I offered him 0.5% of the sales value as incentive, that could amount to double his salary and thus, a good enough incentive. I further laddered the incentive so that he was able to make more as he sold more. I called him back immediately and made this offer to him. He accepted. I reduced my promotion budget by an equivalent amount.

No sooner had I outsourced the job, I started suffering from extreme boredom. I was tempted to seek out marijuana but somehow I forced myself to avoid it. I lapsed back into the cycle of insomnia at nights and headaches during the day. Numerous productive uses of time appeared to me, like reading or exercising or just getting to know more of Malaysia. But it was just not possible with my persistent mental turmoil. I had spent about two months in Singapore and all I had learned was where the clubs were located, which club closed last, which were more reserved and where you could get away with debauchery, which had an ambience more conducive to a sombre mood and where to go if one was feeling frivolous. Here in Malaysia, the situation was no different. Admittedly, I hadn't been to a single club but still, all I had added to my knowledge was the Mamak phenomena and the entire retail store map of Petaling Jaya. It was surely not something that could be used as dinner-time conversation. I inwardly smiled because I knew that I would never do all this just to add to my versatility in handling various dinner conversations. Besides, it would be more entertaining if I were to exercise creativity and manufacture inane topics out of the debris of lies and lean back for a silent laugh as others took the bait.

One particular night, I decided to drive out without a destination in mind, just to see where it took me. After all, I would just be living my life in such a drive. It was around midnight and after negotiating a series of turns and road tolls, I found myself on an expressway which was largely empty. I deliberately avoided looking at the road signs because I didn't want to be influenced by them, and drove on impulse. There were no road lights on this expressway and it looked wonderfully black, with only the small stretch of road in front of me illuminated by my headlights. Miles and miles of road moved under my wheels. I was mesmerised by the white lane markings which originated somewhere in the distance, suddenly infused with life as my car lights shone over it, becoming bigger and bigger as they approached and eventually dying behind me. There were dark, swaying trees all around me to view this magical spectacle but they didn't look impressed. I felt abandoned and decided to abruptly stop the show. The real reason was that it felt criminal to be the God of Light when the whole world was wrapped in darkness. I knew I was one of the privileged few but I was absolutely wasting the privilege. This privilege could not have come without responsibility but someone had failed to deliver the letter stating what was expected of me.

So I switched off the lights. Utter blackness engulfed me. There was nothing to be seen. I drove like this for an indeterminate amount of time. I would have continued like this but I saw lights in the distance and I turned into a nameless town. It also seemed a dead town. I roamed about, passed the police station and the post office and found myself at a dead-end. I killed the engine and got off. There were voices coming from a small alley, just wide enough to allow two to walk together and my feet took me there. A bunch of men, old and young, sat on plastic chairs around a plastic table. They were playing cards. They nodded at me as if they were expecting me and asked if I wanted to join in. I did.

It was a game of poker, Texas Hold'em Poker. I had never played it before. I played a few rounds to acquaint myself with the game but lost everything. My fortunes were still asleep. I was ready to leave when a faceless voice told me, 'That a nice car, mister.' I got his meaning and played one more hand. This time, I was feeling lucky and stupid. It was a dangerously good feeling and I wanted it to last. I played without looking at my cards. One by one, the flop, the turn and the river arrived. When the showdown happened, I couldn't muster the desired cards. I handed over the keys and started the long walk back. I walked till the top of the sun appeared on the horizon. With it, came the traffic and I managed to hitch a ride back to the city. I couldn't believe my luck.

When I woke up, the previous night's events seemed like a distant dream. I went to the parking lot to check if my car was still there but it wasn't. I thanked my stars; now I at least had something to occupy my mind. I tried hard to worry about how I would explain the loss of the car to my employers but however much I tried, I just couldn't bring myself to be concerned. At best, I looked at it as a funny incident. I admired my capacity to look at any and every event from an angle that could make me inwardly smile, sometimes a sad smile but a smile nonetheless. Besides, I had my answer ready. I would just report the car as stolen, and so I did. My rental car company took care of the rest. I was provided with a replacement car in no time at all. I wasn't even required to visit the police station.

I narrated the story to Arjuna when he arrived in Kuala Lumpur on the weekend just before I was due to leave for India but he wasn't impressed. We had just been to a pub where we were rejected by all the women. We blamed it squarely on their racial prejudice against brown skin, although it was more likely that we were simply too direct and brash. We were smoking in the stationary car on the left side of a deserted one-way street near my apartment at the moment. The street was unlit. There was a gas station on our right, which in its present abandoned state could have been a part of a post-apocalyptic world. The moon was only a few days short of its maturity and it cast long shadows on the street, accentuating the mystery and the mood. It was still humid outside and so we barely lowered the windows, to allow a tiny exit for the smoke, while still maintaining a pleasant air-conditioned temperature inside. As a side effect, however, the car was full of smoke now and made for a gloomy interior. I liked it this way. Arjuna opened two cans of beer and passed one to me as he said, 'Till when will you continue to while away your time, mate? It's about time you became more fucking serious.'

I drank a mouthful and asked, 'What happened to you?'

'I am growing up. Look around you. Everybody is.' To my questioning look, he added, 'Bala is engaged to be married. Alex is moving to Greece this week for six months, to revisit his homeland.'

'Dev?'

'His project didn't go too well. He has been posted to India for the time being. But at least he is working hard, not ruining himself like you are.'

'And you?'

He took a drag from his cigarette and threw it away. 'I am moving to Sri Lanka.'

'I thought you said you were never gonna set foot there. What happened?' I offered him another cigarette, lit it for him.

'You mean you don't know? When was the last time you spoke to any of the rest?'

'It's been quite some time, actually.'

'My dad was killed in Colombo about three weeks ago,' he said, in a matter-of-fact tone. I was taken aback and asked, 'How did it happen?'

'There was a police raid. He was at the scene and was killed in the fucking shootout. The police claimed that the people killed were all members of the LTTE.'

'But...', I considered the story, '...you knew your father. You would have known if he was. Won't you?'

'Honestly, we were all taken unawares by the news. I mean, he used to visit Lanka every six months or so. We thought he was just visiting his old friends. But we can't be sure anymore.'

I didn't know what to say and kept quiet. I felt like asking why he hadn't bothered to share this with me but didn't. I would have done the same in his stead. A car zoomed by with blaring loud music. It must have been somebody who had just come of age and was making up for all the lost years tonight. The street fell silent again. Somebody stirred on the left side of the road, further up, possibly a homeless bum or a drunk idiot. The noise had disturbed him.

'So what are you gonna do in Lanka?' I asked.

'This was a fucking wake-up call for me, mate. I think the time has come for me to do what is called for. I am going to fight for the Tamils.'

'LTTE again?'

'Yes.'

'So, you would simply walk up to their admission department, fill out a form, blow a bomb and you would get admission?' The beggar had now got to his feet and was looking around, undecided about what to do.

Arjuna laughed. I liked his laughter, innocent and childlike. 'That's funny. Actually no. Remember the person with whom I was caught and shepherded into jail? His contacts have approached me again. I am sure something will work out.'

'So you are going to wrap explosives around you, walk into a government establishment and blow yourself up? Kill others who have had nothing to do with your father's death? Who are complete strangers?'

He shrugged, 'I'm not gonna kill them myself. I am too valuable to be wasted as a fucking suicide bomber. I will actually be working in the background. I will be an analyst. My job will be to provide intel.'

'And based upon your intel, innocent strangers would be executed.'

'I guess so. That's life.'

'And how would you live with yourself?'

'I think I can carry that burden.' His voice was even.

I looked straight ahead. I was torn between a desire to try and talk Arjuna out of this madness or to simply wish him all the best in pursuing something that he fervently believed in. Though, I wasn't sure if he had thought this through. The beggar was now sifting through the garbage on the street, possibly dehydrated and looking for half-empty water bottles, or maybe even food.

'Prove it to me,' I demanded.

'What?'

'Show me that you can live with the burden of killing a stranger.'

'Of course, I will. In due time.'

'Now,' I insisted.

'How is that possible?' He turned an incredulous look at me.

'It is 3:37 a.m. in the morning. There is a person in front of us on the street; he looks like a homeless loafer. All you have to do is to run him over. Nobody is going to miss him. This is Malaysia and chances are that they would consider it a hit-and-run and leave it at that. Besides, you are flying out tomorrow in any case.'

'Are you fucking nuts? I am not going to kill him. He hasn't done anything to me.'

'Your future victims also would not have done anything to you or your family. Hell, they won't even know you,' I said.

'Besides, I told you I won't be killing them myself. There is a difference. You may not understand that but I do.'

I considered his line of argument. 'Okay then. Order me. I will run him over.'

'What?'

'Just give me your word and I will run him over. That way, I would have killed him but the responsibility will still lie with you. I want to see if you can do that. If you can, then no amount of convincing otherwise will stop you from joining the LTTE.'

He looked at me for some time. In the darkness, I couldn't make out his facial expression. I sensed that he needed one last push. 'Be honest. Even you are not sure if you can live with murders, be it for a cause or not. Here is a chance for you to find out.' I seemed to have struck the right chord. He nodded.

'You have to say it,' I told him and he whispered, 'Just fucking do it.'

The engine roared furiously like it knew that it was going to taste blood. I imagined the gas-station had come alive to watch this event. Even the moon defied the laws of physics and stayed on for a few more dying moments. I switched to the driving gear. The car moved forward. I got in line with the beggar before flooring the accelerator. Eight hundred kilogrammes of metal and rubber gained momentum as the seat gripped my back. Arjuna held the dashboard with both his hands. We were about to hit him when two things happened simultaneously. Arjuna shouted 'Stop' in a drowning man's voice and the beggar sensed the approaching car and moved sideways to avoid it. The car hit him on his side and he went down. I pressed the brakes and the car screeched to a halt. Burnt rubber fumes engulfed us. Behind, the beggar was rolling on the road trying to get up. I put the car in the reverse gear and asked Arjuna, 'Are you sure?' He was sobbing. 'Don't do it. Please don't do it.'

We took the bleeding beggar to the nearby hospital. I concocted a story about an accident. Arjuna offered to pay the entire medical bill.

Arjuna left unceremoniously in the morning before I woke up. He didn't even bother to leave a note. I couldn't quite understand his behaviour in the morning or mine of the night, for that matter. Over the years, I have often indulged in introspection about my behaviour, in a structured manner, as Alex would have done. Starting with the motive: was it just a gimmick to prove my superiority to another human being or was it a stupid move to prove I was different? I have persuaded myself that my motive was indeed honourable. I genuinely wanted to ensure that Arjuna knew what he was doing, or going to do. To my surprise, I found I honestly didn't know or care what the right thing was, as long as Arjuna believed it to be so. This eventually led me to the horrifying conclusion that I wouldn't have given a damn if that beggar had died that night. If he hadn't ducked, he would have been dead. I have often felt deeply ashamed of myself but then I'd ask myself again, was it really as it seemed? Was it he who had ducked to the left or was it me who had steered the car, however slightly, to the right? I couldn't be sure if it was just my mind justifying what otherwise was a demonic act. I hadn't known back then if Arjuna would change his decision but it felt fulfilling that he knew just what he was walking into.

•◆

17

Game Over

My stay in Malaysia ended and I landed back at Mumbai airport. I had a sense of déjà vu when I hailed an autorickshaw from the airport to the same apartment that I had arrived at about four months ago. It seemed like an era had passed. I lit a cigarette in the autorickshaw and lapsed into my favourite pastime of analysing the past. I could call my stay in Malaysia partly successful. While I didn't manage to hit my sales target, my review was still above average. My boss had told me, just short of officially confirming it, that I could count on a successful career in this company. I had managed to stop doing drugs and, good or bad, I had largely led a solitary life of abstinence. What a contradiction it was from the life of indulgence in Singapore. And yet, despite living life on both sides of the continuum, I still couldn't come to terms with the superficiality or pointlessness of my job. I had continued to play the fool in the same manner that I had done in Singapore, and it was only a miracle that I had been able to get the job confirmation. One thing was clear to me: I wasn't cut out for a corporate career. But what was there for me to do besides this? It wasn't like I had any other qualification or that I was equipped to do something different. Perhaps my expectations from a job were too demanding. After all, it wasn't a perfect world that I was living in. Perhaps Alex was right in looking at a job as a means to achieve a bigger end.

I had to ring the bell a number of times before I remembered that I still had the key. I extracted it from my bag and unlocking the door, entered the house. It looked more inviting than I remembered. Perhaps it was because the previous occupants, the interns, would have vacated the place, having finished their training. It felt good to have the whole apartment to myself. I went straight to the master bedroom and laid out my luggage there. I felt the urge to take off my clothes and to roam around naked but I resisted it. I found a can of beer in the fridge and sat down by the window, the breeze blowing through my long hair. There was someone coughing in the other room and momentarily, I wondered if there was an intruder in the house. I got up and opened the door to that room only to realise that Dev was still here. He was sitting on the floor using the bed as backrest, the quintessential cigarette, or was it a joint, in his right hand, which itself was lying lifelessly by his side. The floor was not the usual pearl-coloured one but was spotted dark red because of the blood gushing out of his wrist. He looked up at me with droopy eyes and said, 'I wasn't really expecting you.'

'Do you want me to call the ambulance?' I said, wondering what I had done to land up in such a situation when all I was looking for was to have a smoke and go to bed.

'Not really. I intended it to be the way it is. Your presence is the only unplanned element,' he replied, taking a puff. 'You probably want to know what led to all this, don't you?'

'Don't let me force my presence on you. It is alright if you want to be alone at this moment. If I were in your position, I would have preferred to be alone, but then you are not me,' I replied, suddenly conscious of these being the last moments of his life and thus, offering him the courtesy of letting him decide what he wanted to do. It was a surreal moment.

'If it were any other person, I would have probably gone to the extent of killing him to have my solitude. But you are alright. The very fact that you asked me if I wanted to be rescued suggests your absolute reluctance to intrude on the moment. I like that,' he said, mistaking for compassion my selfish intention to avoid doing anything at this late hour. 'Take a seat where I can see you.'

I dragged a chair from the living room and made myself comfortable. It all still felt surreal.

'I actually feel good to have a conversation with somebody. There are so many things that I want to explain but I may not have enough time. Maybe I will explain this relinquishing act first. I was told today that I am not good enough to join this firm. You see, a lot of things would have come together if only they had offered me the job. This job was like the foundation stone, and a lot of things that really mattered were perched atop it. I would have been able to make up with my girlfriend of so many years, get back again with her. My mother would not have had to continue working even in this old age and most importantly, I would have regained my confidence in myself.'

'But those fuckers didn't really care about all that. They collectively decided that I am unworthy of kissing their smelly asses. I was so close to patching up with my girl but what does she say when I break the news to her? She told me that I am a loser and will always remain one. But that is still fine. If she can't support me in these bad times, then she is probably not worth it. But the thing that I dread most is going back home and facing my friends, my uncles and my cousins. Hell, I can't even bear to face you guys. Didn't Bala say that you have to be really pathetic not to be able to make it?' He paused as if replaying Bala's statement in his mind. 'And what would really kill me is the look on my mother's face, a look full of misery that has increasingly become more resigned with every failure that I bring onto her. So, my friend, here I am, having slit my wrist.' He was still as articulate as ever, though he was now slurring a bit. 'Do you mind rolling a joint for me? My hands aren't exactly what they used to be.'

'Of course. Anything for you, though I may not be too good at it.' I dragged the polythene containing the cigarette paper and the weed towards me. 'By the way, in my books, slitting wrists is quite a good way to go. It is slow, involves just the right amount of pain and gives you enough time to appreciate the so-called near-death experience, the gradual spreading of darkness, until you are gone. Well, that is how I imagine it, in any case.'

'You know when I cut myself, I thought about who might miss me afterwards. The only person who would probably realise my absence will be my mum and she doesn't really expect me back home for another week. And I suddenly realised that it might be days before somebody notices that I am missing and that too, only because of the rotting smell of my decomposing body. That was when you walked into the room. Urban living is serious business. Hell, I don't even know what is going on next door. Who has had a bad day at office? Who is cutting his or her birthday cake alone at this very moment? Who is having sex and who is jerking off? Who is trying on his mother's undergarments and who is getting raped? Hell, I don't even know how many people in this city might be travelling with me tonight. You can't even choose a time and be sure of dying alone nowadays.' His words were running into each other. I lit the joint and passed it to him. He grabbed it like it was the last link connecting him to this world and inhaled deeply. 'How would you have liked to go?'

'I don't know. But at gun-point, I would pick jumping off a cliff top, a really tall cliff at that,' I said.

'Why….?' He was almost dozing.

'Why what?'

'Huh?' He woke up like he had been asleep for a long time. 'Oh yeah. Why the free- fall?'

'Sometimes I feel what I miss most is freedom. Don't confuse it with the freedom of speech and other similar concepts. Here, I refer to the absolute freedom of doing anything you want to do, living life without worrying about taxes and rentals, laws – moral or otherwise, parents' clutches, girlfriend's vibes, social categorisation, worrying where your next meal is going to come from. At other times, I feel that the best times of my life were when I was a small town boy, living with my parents, bound for a mediocre, predetermined life of marrying, having kids and slogging throughout my life for their well-being. And that once I moved out of that zone, my life has been falling vertically, with absolutely no vision of any impending doom. And all this while, the speed of the fall has been increasing at an exponential rate. Sometimes, it feels that I am more likely to go off in a final blast of energy rather than see the bottom.' I took the joint, inhaled deeply and wondered what the point of talking about all this was. 'Either way, jumping off the cliff seems to be the best way but not yet.'

'So unfair,' he complained.

'What is?'

'You are. It has all…come so easily…to you. You go to the best school. Get the nicest job. You probably are the best among your peers. And the, what's the word…' He raked his numb brain. 'Yeah, irony…the irony is that you don't even want any of this. In fact, you go out of your way to create misery in perfect circumstances.' He paused again, this time for a long time. 'And here I am. If I could even have half of what you have had, my life would have been so different and worthwhile. It is all so cruel.'

'I don't know what to say to that. I guess we all have to find our own destination and while one destination may be relevant in your point of view, it may not be that important in my point of view.'

'Ah. So you think I am a lesser mortal? Somebody to be pitied upon but not to be considered equal?'

'Hang on. What I said didn't come out right. What I meant was that it is all relative. The destination itself is relatively more absolute than the traveller. The traveller, in his turn, and in this age, is so influenced by his fellow passengers that he himself is not sure of what he really wants. It all boils down to what makes one happy. And that is so ephemeral a concept that it will wither away if one so much as whispers it.'

He pondered over this for a long time, his head swaying in a circular anticlockwise fashion as if digesting the thought while at a loss of words to respond with. 'So you think….' He broke off, continued moving his head and finally stopped, with his gaze fixed on a particular pearly spot amid the red on the floor. 'You think I am influenced by my peers and don't have a personal, definite concept of what I want?'

'Maybe you did or didn't. Assuming you did, there is nothing wrong in wanting what you wanted, assuming that would have made you happy. In my case, that doesn't make me happy and it is solely because we are different people and are bound to have different destinies. In fact, I would have so loved to swap with you so at least I would have had tangible objectives and wouldn't have to face the tiring prospect of constantly untangling my conflicted feelings.'

'I wish we had this conversation before. So we both want to be in the other's shoes. And yet here I am slitting my wrists and there you are, about to jump off a cliff. We are both fucked.'

I didn't think I would have ever jumped off a cliff but I didn't want to contradict him and make him feel even more miserable. The floor around Dev was now a crude crimson and from the direction of its flow, it threatened to touch my toes fairly soon. Dev's head slung over his left shoulder and he looked like the resigned and weary passenger on a Mumbai local who knew he had a long way to go but couldn't hasten the process any further. He suddenly woke up with a jerk as if something flashed through his mind, 'You didn't reply to my e-mails.'

'I should have. It was just that I was too preoccupied with my own problems. But that is no real excuse. I guess I was just selfish and couldn't be bothered with them.'

'You know, I thought I had a special bond with you. You were like me, except luckier. I thought you could have helped me.'

'I didn't know you needed help. Your e-mails were all so carefree that I thought you were having a nice time,' I was lying; I had noticed from his e-mails the undercurrent of a person going over the edge. I just hadn't realised that it was for real.

Dev had dozed off again, this time for the last time. His head hung forward, directly between his shoulder blades and his chin pointed down to his navel. His left hand was resting peacefully on his thigh while his other hand still held the now dead joint. I had a sickly wet feeling deep within, originating from my feet and spreading to the rest of the body before it decidedly took over. My toes were now covered in Dev's wasted blood but I didn't move them. I wanted to be tortured. I wanted to turn the Yellow Pages and be lucky enough to stumble upon the classified advertisement of a torture specialist. I wanted to call him over, pay him handsomely to pull out my nails and whatever else he could do to a human body without actually killing the person. But that would have been the easier way out. What I was going through now was the real torture. All my senses screamed at me to do something. But I just couldn't move. What was it that Dev had said? Yeah, that I could have helped him. I could have been a little less self-occupied. I could have saved him. But, could I really have? What possible advice could I have given him that might have persuaded him otherwise? I couldn't possibly be made responsible for his fate. Besides, didn't he himself make light of all his sufferings, almost to the point of having us believe he revelled in adverse circumstances? Didn't he act as if he considered himself privileged to have a challenging life ahead of him, and that he wouldn't have it any other way?

I wondered if he was still alive but I hadn't the nerve to check. Maybe his spirit was desperately trying to break free of the material bonds or maybe it had but was still around, inspecting me curiously. Could it read my thoughts? I sat there for a long time; at least it seemed a long time. I waited patiently, without moving a muscle, to ensure that he was dead before I moved. Was it a few minutes or a couple of hours, I did not know. But I had to see his face. Something told me that my answers lay in his face but I was petrified to look at it while I was unsure if he was really dead. What if he grabbed my throat and strangled me? Oh, that would have been merciful. But what if he smiled at me, that knowing, condescending smile? That would surely replace my recurring nightmare of being strangled with an even more horrendous nightmare. Actually, I instinctively knew. He was gone. My dreams would now solely comprise of his smiling face as he raised his hands to show me his cut wrists, with blood gushing out animatedly. And in my dreams, I would be sitting on this very armchair, unable to move a limb. I would want to shout but no sound would come out of my throat. I would want to move but my feet would be firmly glued to the floor. I would look down and see his auburn blood holding my feet in a vice-like grip. I would be able to see it spreading its tentacles and consuming me. I shuddered.

Eventually I got up to look at his face but my cowardly feet took me out of the room as if they had a mind of their own. I left a bloodied trail behind me all the way to the window by which I sat down yet again. I wished that it was all a dream and that I might have just come into the apartment, having my customary cigarette before bedtime and that everything was normal. But it wasn't. Outside was a blue-black sky without the hint of a star. I lit a cigarette and recalled what Dev had once said about smoking – that it was an inspiring moment of self-realisation. Or was it me who had said that? It didn't matter. I marvelled at what a glamorous loser he was. They all were. Bala and Arjuna. Heck, even Alex was like that. They were homeless wanderers, nomads; some wandering over the edge while some were lucky, as they had glimpsed the dawn before anybody else. What was extraordinary was that their first impulse had always been to go over the edge, to self-destruct. There must be something in our genes surviving from the prehistoric age, forcing us to behave in this manner. Or was it a futile attempt to think more of ourselves than we really were – an iota in a tiny speck on the grand cosmic plane of time and space. Why couldn't one come to terms with one's miniscule stature and live one's life as a gift and not as drudgery?

I blew the smoke out. It momentarily hung there taking advantage of the wind's indecision. It slowly went up, changed its mind and then it went down in a spiralling manner, before gathering speed and finally exploding in my face. I waited for the inspiring self-realisation but none came forth. I threw the cigarette out. I stood and looked out the window, supporting myself on the railing. It looked inviting. I looked down and saw the darkness spread vast and wide. This was my moment of reckoning. Here was my chance to redeem myself. All I needed to do was walk out of the window, into nothing. And then I could explain to Dev in the after-world all that had remained unsaid. But before that, I had to face my demons and look into Dev's face. For, this was not my decision. This was Dev's decision and he had already made it for me before he departed, etched in his face. It was just me delaying the moment. I prayed to God to give me courage.

I went back into the room and sat in the same armchair I had sat in, before. I carefully placed my feet on the same spot, so as not to disturb this sacred shrine till such time as I considered myself worthy enough. I considered my options. I had come to accept by now that Dev's departure was my fault. I had finally committed a murder. Just a few days ago, I had almost murdered a stranger in cold blood but thankfully, he had survived. Now I had accomplished it, though with regret. I justified to myself that the first attempted murder was to rescue Arjuna and I had succeeded in doing so. Even though I might have lost a good friend, I lived with the knowledge that he was on the right path. However, in the present instance, there was no consolation for me. The time for that was long gone because I had missed that turn. Then again, I had a feeling that something had indeed been salvaged here. It could have been me. All I had to do was to face it in that resting face of Dev. And so I got up and against my comfort, I stepped into oodles of sticky liquid soundlessly. I went down on my knees in front of the dead man. I raised his chin with my index finger so his face was level with mine, only inches away. I saw in his face, understanding and forgiveness. I also saw something else, a glimpse of hope, hope for the rest of us and immediately it was all crystal clear to me. I was rescued but I would carry this burden for the rest of my life. It was a curse but a liberating curse, far more preferable to anything else. For I knew what I had to do, however difficult it might be. I swore that I would do whatever it took to show the light to others like me, others like Dev, others like Arjuna, others like Bala. I would be a potent combination of sufficient childishness and sufficient wisdom, and would inspire others to face their inner torment and to find what truly defined them. I would show them that the meaning they sought resided within them. The eternal traveller was dead.

Epilogue

Now, I am back in the present and I am looking out at the deserted street through the window of my room. It has just rained, making for a green view. The water has just about cleared but the road is still wet. The sun should be coming out any minute now and so will the small kids from the school on the right. Perhaps in the evening, I will go for a walk in the park but not before I have had my afternoon tea.

It had been quite a nightmare trying to convince the police authorities about my lack of involvement in Dev's suicide. It didn't help that my toes and knees were smeared with his blood and that it was fairly obvious that I had smoked in Dev's room. I had explained to them that I had seen him only in the morning and in my bewildered state, I hadn't realised that I was stepping into his blood. Further, that I had smoked in the same room to calm myself down. Thankfully, the officer-in-charge was an old acquaintance, the one who had once threatened to lock me up over a false police report, and he let me go.

I am very much in touch with others and this time around, through my own effort. Alex is presently based in Spain, with the same company. He loves his job and is proud of how it allows him to live in various countries and be exposed to various cultures. Although, I secretly think that the real reason is the opportunity to bed beauties from all over the world. He proudly calls himself 'a global citizen'. He hasn't changed his ways but maintains that the six months spent in Greece were an eye-opener for him. His next destination is somewhere in Latin America and by his own confession, he believes that he will come out married from there, so beautiful does he find the Latinas.

Bala is blissfully married and lives in Mumbai. She has changed jobs and is doing well in her career as well, but she has firmly put her personal life ahead of her career. Her mother and sister stay with her. She is thinking of expanding her family soon. She has already thought of names for them. A daughter will be named 'Ala' while a son will be named 'Chet'. Creativity was never really her forte.

Despite my best attempts at making contact, I heard from Arjuna only after a long time. He has continued in the same job and is currently based in Sydney. His mother has also moved in with him and they attempt to move on after their grave loss. He has revived his radio-show for curry immigrants and is trying to get a deal for a TV show. We carefully refrain from mentioning that night between us or to anybody else, for that matter. I think that he still secretly blames me for Dev's untimely demise but I have a feeling that he will come around, given enough time. He is going to spend this coming Deepawali with me in Jaipur. I just hope he doesn't attempt to blow up any buildings.

As for your humble narrator, I have carved out a successful career in Mumbai with the same company. I have developed ethics of late and work diligently nowadays, for the most part at least. I even wrote a letter to Zul thanking him for being such an inspiring role model and also listing down top ten sales tips that I learnt from him. I have a feeling, though, that he still prefers his company watch to my letter.

The accomplishment I am most proud about, however, has been the academy I have set up in Jaipur, where I spend the summer every year conducting road-shows and walk-in-for-career-advice sessions. When I had mentioned this idea casually to Rashmi, she set in motion a chain of discussions which led to numerous employees donating to this venture and culminated into David promising to match all such contributions. Sometimes, I wonder why my perception about the company initially was so selectively cynical and I blame it on my prejudiced mindset. Bala proved to me that people can change and so I have. And contrary to my previous belief that change can only be triggered by a significant life-changing event, I have come to realise that all it really needs is the right opportunity. In fact, whether an event is an opportunity or not is determined by whether a person is internally ready for the change.

The academy's administration head is my father. It is called, in Dev's memory, 'Resident Dormitus.'

www.ingramcontent.com/pod-product-compliance
Lightning Source LLC
Chambersburg PA
CBHW030233170426
43201CB00006B/201